WALKS

LINCOLNSHIRE

HUGH MARROWS

BRADWELL
BOOKS

WALKS FOR ALL AGES

LINCOLNSHIRE

HUGH MARROWS

BRADWELL
BOOKS

Published by Bradwell Books
9 Orgreave Close Sheffield S13 9NP
Email: books@bradwellbooks.co.uk
© Hugh Marrows 2013

The right of Hugh Marrows as author of this work has been asserted by him in accordance with the Copyright, Design and Patents Act, 1988. All rights reserved. No part of this publication may be produced, stored in a retrieval system or transmitted in any form or by any means, electronic, mechanical, photocopying, recording or otherwise without the prior permission of Bradwell Books.
British Library Cataloguing in Publication Data: a catalogue record for this book is available from the British Library.

1st Edition

ISBN: 9781902674520

Print: Gomer Press, Llandysul, Ceredigion SA44 4JL

Design by: Erik Siewko Creative, Derbyshire.
eriksiewko@gmail.com

Photograph Credits: © Hugh Marrows

Maps: Contain Ordnance Survey data © Crown copyright and database right 2013

The information in this book has been produced in good faith and is intended as a general guide. Bradwell Books and its authors have made all reasonable efforts to ensure that the details are correct at the time of publication. Bradwell Books and the author cannot accept any responsibility for any changes that have taken place subsequent to the book being published. It is the responsibility of individuals undertaking any of the walks listed in this publication to exercise due care and consideration for the health and well being of each other in the party. Particular care should be taken if you are inexperienced. The walks in this book are not especially strenuous but individuals taking part should ensure they are fit and able to complete the walk before setting off.

CONTENTS

Walk 1.	Ancaster	p. 8
Walk 2.	Barton - on - Humber	p. 12
Walk 3.	Billingborough	p. 16
Walk 4.	Biscathorpe & Gayton le Wold	p. 20
Walk 5.	Boston & Anton's Gowt	p. 24
Walk 6.	Culverthorpe	p. 28
Walk 7.	Frampton Marsh	p. 32
Walk 8.	Hagworthingham, Snipe Dales & Winceby	p. 36
Walk 9.	Haxey	p. 42
Walk 10.	Heighington & Branston	p. 46
Walk 11.	Lincoln (Uphill)	p. 52
Walk 12.	South & North Rauceby	p. 56
Walk 13.	Tattershall & Coningsby	p. 62
Walk 14.	Tealby & Tealby Thorpe	p. 66
Walk 15.	Tetney Lock & Humber Bank	p. 70
Walk 16.	The Deepings	p. 74
Walk 17.	Thornton Abbey	p. 78
Walk 18.	Thurlby & Dole Wood	p. 82
Walk 19.	Well & Rigsby	p. 86
Walk 20.	Woolsthorpe & Stenwith	p. 92

INTRODUCTION

Welcome to "Walks for All Ages" in Lincolnshire. These twenty walks have been specially chosen for family groups – the longest being a fraction over 6 miles and with several routes having both longer and shorter options. The choice of routes also attempts to introduce readers to the wide variety of scenery that makes up this large county – from north to south and from the coast to the hills of the Wolds.

Many have attractions along the way that will interest children including historic sites, museums and nature reserves etc The "Basics" panel accompanying each route will help you choose walks within your family's abilities and you can always work up to longer ones as your experience develops. Note too that the "Start Point" information gives a postcode for satellite navigation users – although in a few cases, where this is in the open countryside, these may be only approximate.

Footwear should be strong and waterproof as there is inevitably uneven ground and there are short distances over arable land on some routes. Older walkers might like to consider using walking poles.

Readers should remember too that the countryside is a changing environment. The route guides are as accurate as we can make them but footpaths are sometimes re-routed and there can be changes where new stiles or kissing/bridle gates are set up. Also, nowadays some country pubs are unfortunately closing down (though occasionally some re-open again), so it's wise to check before setting off if you are depending on them for refreshments.

The route guides and maps should get you round these walks without difficulty but I find that it is always advisable to have an Ordnance Survey map available if possible – the relevant Explorer sheet is best. These larger scale maps contain greater detail and may assist in locating the start points more easily. We have used grid references in the "Basics" panel too and the use of this helpful – even essential – map-reading skill is easily learnt as all OS maps give an explanatory example. It's always useful to know where you are – to plan an alternative route in an emergency, for example!

Adults with pets or children with them should be mindful too of the hazards of roads (even quiet country lanes) and water features where these are present on the walks. You will almost certainly at some time find meadows with sheep and lambs or cattle in them – please take care when there are calves about – and

WALKS FOR ALL AGES - LINCOLNSHIRE

this is one time when dogs must be on a leash or under very close control.

The given — perhaps we should say estimated — walk times are just that: estimates! Readers will know their own limitations best and some will be quicker than others. You will therefore still to need to allow additional time for any rests, picnics, pub meals, photography etc.

I must also express my thanks to those landlords of inns who have kindly consented to readers using their car parks as a starting point. Do show your appreciation by popping in — even if only for crisps and a drink.

And — last but not least — please always remember, and follow, the Country Code! Remember too that the countryside you are visiting is someone else's home or workplace; so don't spoil it for those who follow in your footsteps!

Happy rambling!

ANCASTER

For this short walk we explore the Lincolnshire Wildlife Trust's nature reserve in "The Valley" just outside Ancaster village.

Ancaster straddles Ermine Street, a major road built by the Romans to link London with York as they extended their AD 43 invasion into northern England. Ancaster also lies close to the Jurassic Way, a prehistoric trackway following the spine of high ground through central and eastern England. Its name derives from the geological Jurassic period whose rocks predominate along its route. Locally, to the north of the village, it is known as Pottergate.

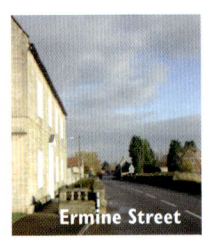

Ermine Street

Make time, before or after the walk, to visit St Martin's Church, whose dedication is to a Roman soldier who converted to Christianity. The church has another Roman link too for it stands on a former Roman temple site, and near the gate three small statues of fertility goddesses are set into the churchyard wall. Also inside is an exhibition about Roman Ancaster.

St Martin's Church

Hugh of Avalon, who became Bishop of Lincoln in 1186, was in London when he died in 1200 but was returned to Lincoln for burial and before reaching the city his cortege made its last overnight resting place in Ancaster church. A chapel is therefore dedicated to him and contains an altar carved from local Ancaster limestone. Hugh was made a saint in 1220.

Geologists are not entirely certain how "The Valley" nature reserve was formed but the consensus of opinion is that it was by erosion from glacial meltwater during the last ice age – hence its steep sides. (Local geology is explained in more detail on the "Geology" information board on the village trail. See below.) "The Valley" was acquired by the Lincolnshire Wildlife Trust in 1982 and they have since cleared away much overgrown scrubland to create one of the finest limestone grassland habitats

Roman Stone Coffin *Pasque Flowers* *Entrance to The Valley*

WALKS FOR ALL AGES - LINCOLNSHIRE

in the county, which now supports a wide variety of limestone-loving flowers. These include the rare spring-flowering pasqueflower, many orchids as well as numerous insect species. There is more information on the reserve notice board and the Trust's website.

At the start and finish of the walk we pass the site of the Roman township. It was located in the meadow immediately across the road from the church and abundant archaeological finds have included many coin hoards. Indeed they were of such quantity that Arthur Mee in his "King's England — Lincolnshire" book, relates how 18th-century villagers used them locally as currency.

In the cemetery behind the church there are two massive Roman stone coffins — worth going to see! The cemetery is also familiar to botanists for being one of only two sites in the country where Tall Thrift — a relation of Sea Pink — can be found. But how can they be so certain?

The Valley - Upper Path

THE BASICS

Distance in miles & km: 2 miles: 3.25 km. (Village trail extra)
Gradient: Gentle ascent and descent to "The Valley" is by steps.
Severity: Easy.
Approx time to walk: 60 mins.
Stiles: None.
Maps: OS Landranger 130 (Grantham): Explorer 247.
Path description: Pavements, firm footpaths and grassland.
Start Point: Outside Ancaster church. NG32 3GW (GR 984434)
Parking: Roadside parking outside church or in village.
Dog friendly: On a lead in the nature reserve; sheep grazing.
Public toilets: Only at the inn.
Nearest food: The Ermine inn, Ancaster.

ANCASTER WALK

Readers may also like to do the village's own Heritage Trail, which can easily be added to this walk and involves only an extra mile in distance. It is self-guided and not detailed in the route instruction below but begins at the village hall close to the junction of Ermine Street and Wilsford Lane; not far from the inn. Each of its eight information boards provides onward instructions to the next. They discuss such matters as local geology, wildlife and history; including the Romans, of course, whose small garrison here was called Causennae. The trail ends back at the church.

The Lincolnshire Wildlife Trust also has

Ermine Inn

another nature reserve at Ancaster. The village Heritage trail passes Moor Closes, a sixteen-acre reserve that includes important wet meadow and marshland habitats and has a short visitor trail.

Roman Legion Standard

1. Stand with your back to the church, cross the road and turn right towards the traffic lights. At the crossroads go left a few yards along the pavement until you can cross (carefully) to a continuing pavement on the other side. A few yards further on turn right into the entrance of "The Valley" nature reserve.

2. A short track leads to the entrance gate, just before which a gently rising footpath branches off to the left. Take this and continue for about half a mile to a three-way footpath sign.

3. Go down the steps to your right to reach "The Valley" bottom and then bear right along the valley floor until you reach the entrance gate again. Now retrace your steps back to the church.

The Valley Nature Reserve

WALKS FOR ALL AGES - LINCOLNSHIRE

KEY

- START POINT ●
- CROSSING ✗
- CHURCH †

4. To finish your walk go through the churchyard into the lane behind it. The cemetery is now 100 yards to your right. After seeing the two Roman coffins return the way you came.

11

BARTON - ON - HUMBER

This easy walk explores the ancient port of Barton-on-Humber, Lincolnshire's most northerly town, to see some of its fascinating buildings. It begins on the Humber bank at the award-winning Waters' Edge Nature Reserve.

Historically Barton depended upon the Humber and shipping to generate its wealth and was already an important port when the Domesday Book was compiled in 1086. The town's long history has, as you might expect, created an extremely varied architectural legacy.

Visitor Centre

One important geological factor in Barton's development was the riverbank clay deposits, ideal for brick and tile making, an industry that contributed to the town's prosperity for several centuries as well as adding to its visual appeal and that of the surrounding area. In recent years the abandoned and now flooded claypits beside the Humber have been transformed into nature reserves or converted for use as leisure activities such as sailing and fishing.

Humber Bridge

The most recently opened reserve is the Waters' Edge, a 110-acre country park created on an old chemical works site. The ultra-modern visitor centre was designed on "green" architectural principles, both in its method of construction and in the materials used. A terrace café overlooks the lagoons with their abundant wildlife and the visitor centre has maps of various colour-coded walking routes within the reserve.

Nearby are the picturesque wharves of Barton Haven, now somewhat silted up, which once formed the town's old port and boat-building yards. The footbridge spanning the Haven leads to the Humber Bridge viewing area. Also nearby is the amazing 450-yard long Ropewalk built in 1767. This now contains art and craft galleries and a display about the history of rope making, once another important local industry.

Water's Edge Nature Reserve

Barton Haven

WALKS FOR ALL AGES - LINCOLNSHIRE

There is a café there too!

After leaving the nature reserve our walk explores some of Barton's characterful narrow streets. The town's best-known features are of course its two magnificent churches, St Mary's and St Peter's, standing only a few yards apart on slightly elevated ground. St Mary's boasts a remarkable mixture of architectural styles from around 1150 onwards. Begun as a chapel of ease, now with centuries of alterations and additions it still stands testimony to Barton's former wealth and prominence.

Architecturally St Peter's is perhaps the more interesting of the two for it is one of England's finest Saxon churches, being some two centuries older than its neighbour. The tower is characteristic of the mid-10th century, a time when building in stone rather than wood was an innovation. As a consequence stonemasons were still experimenting in adapting woodworking techniques and this is clearly illustrated by the mitred masonry joints on the tower. Redundant since 1972, St Peter's is cared for by English Heritage (their website gives opening times etc.).

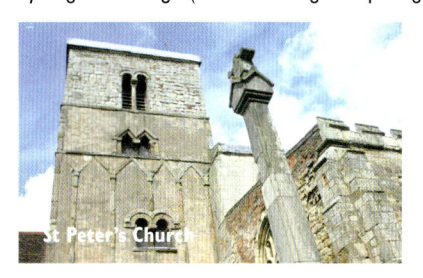

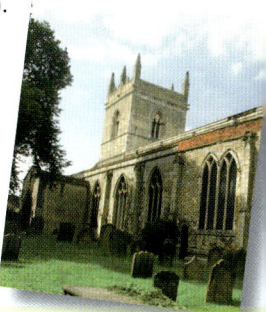

St Peter's Church

THE BASICS

Distance in miles & km: 2¾ miles: 4.5 kilometres.
Gradient: gentle ascent into town.
Severity: Easy.
Approx time to walk: 75 mins.
Stiles: None.
Maps: OS Landranger 112: Explorer 281.
Path description: Surfaced paths in nature reserve. Town pavements.
Start Point: Waters Edge Visitor Centre. DN18 5JR (GR 031234)
Parking: Free at Waterside Country Park.
Dog friendly: On leads throughout.
Public toilets: At Waterside Visitor Centre.
Nearest food: Waterside Visitor Centre; The Ropery; or in Barton.

BARTON - ON - HUMBER WALK

Nearby is a huge windmill (situated near the Market Place) built in 1810 to grind not grain but local chalk for use in starch and paint.

The railway arrived in Barton in 1849 as a 3½-mile-long, single-track, branch line from New Holland. It was built by the Manchester, Sheffield and Lincolnshire Railway following their takeover of the Humber ferries, and the Great Grimsby and Sheffield Junction Railway that operated them. There are two additional options for readers still with energy to spare. Visit the Lincolnshire Wildlife Trust reserve at Far Ings (along Far Ings Road, off Waterside) or, as a complete contrast,

Burgate, Barton-on-Humber

stroll across the pedestrian walkway of the Humber Bridge, accessed from near the bridge viewing area. All in all Barton offers much to see and do on a day out!

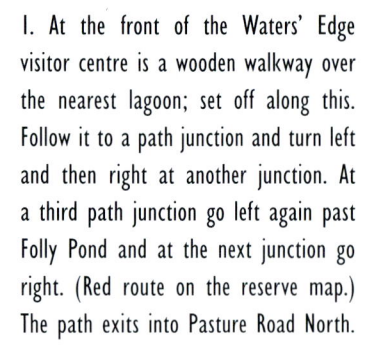

Barton Haven

1. At the front of the Waters' Edge visitor centre is a wooden walkway over the nearest lagoon; set off along this. Follow it to a path junction and turn left and then right at another junction. At a third path junction go left again past Folly Pond and at the next junction go right. (Red route on the reserve map.) The path exits into Pasture Road North.

2. Turn right over the railway and at the junction of Falkland Way and Pasture Road keep ahead (i.e. up Pasture Road.) Pass the end of Butts Road and continue uphill, then as the road begins to bend right cross over and climb the steps into St Peter's churchyard.

3. Leave the churchyard by turning right down the sloping path beyond the tower and cross the road again into Burgate to visit St Mary's church. (You could now look at some of Barton on your own – the area around Preistgate and the Market Place are worth exploring – then return to Burgate.) Keep ahead past St Mary's, walking ahead along Burgate and continuing as it becomes High Street. On reaching the junction with Hungate bear right and go right again down Fleetgate to emerge opposite the station.

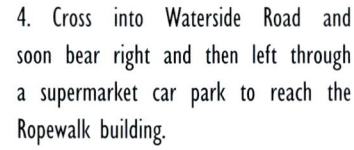

4. Cross into Waterside Road and soon bear right and then left through a supermarket car park to reach the Ropewalk building.

WALKS FOR ALL AGES - LINCOLNSHIRE

KEY
- START POINT — ●
- CROSSING — ✕
- CHURCH — ✝
- VISITOR CENTRE — V

Barton-on-Humber

Barton Haven

Butts Road

Holydyke

BARTON-U

St Peter's Ch

5. A footpath to the right of the Ropewalk leads back to the Waters' Edge.

15

BILLINGBOROUGH

This walk visits the site of a long-lost mediaeval priory founded by St Gilbert of Sempringham.

It was at Sempringham that Lincolnshire's "home-grown" saint was born around 1083. St Gilbert was a knight's son, born deformed and educated in France. Once back in Sempringham about 1139 he founded his own rather unusual monastic "Gilbertine" order that accepted both men and women and eventually established thirteen priories. The one at Sempringham, dissolved in 1538, lay to the south of the present church. St Gilbert died on 4th February 1189 and was canonised in 1202.

Sempringham Church

The earthworks visible on the priory site are those of a later mansion built by Lord Clinton, Earl of Lincoln, an admiral in Queen Elizabeth I's navy. The present-day church (St Andrew's) retains its Norman doorway and a 13th-century south door. One unusual feature is the Holy Well at the bottom of the churchyard. The site of the mediaeval village lies under the surrounding fields.

St Andrew's Church

There are Welsh links with Sempringham too through its association with Princess Gwenllian, a daughter of Prince Llywelyn. Regarded by Edward I as a threat in Wales she was "exiled" to Sempringham aged one, remaining there until her death in 1337 – aged fifty-four! The Princess Gwenllian Society has erected a memorial to her and an information board in both English and Welsh.

At the time of the Domesday Book the hamlet of Birthorpe had eight freemen and eight smallholders (plus their families) so was probably a bigger settlement than it is now. As you pass through, note the 18th-century Manor House and an old barn with a "VR 1855" plaque.

We conclude our walk in Billingborough with its variety of old buildings. Look out for the former railway station (1871), the old fire station (1890), Billingborough Hall (1620) and, most picturesque of all, Church Farm (17th century). Here is another St

WALKS FOR ALL AGES - LINCOLNSHIRE

Andrew's, whose slender 150-feet-high spire overlooks the nearby millennium sundial and springs.

Incidentally, on the field sections of the shorter route to Birthorpe watch out for fragments of pottery as scraps of old roof tiles etc. are occasionally ploughed up.

Note that Billingborough car park is in West Road (behind the fire station).

17th centrury Church Farm

The Old Fire Station

THE BASICS

Distance in miles & km: 4 or 4¾ miles: 6.5 or 7.5 kilometres.
Gradient: Virtually level; very gentle ascents and descents.
Severity: Easy.
Approx time to walk: 120 mins.
Stiles: None.
Maps: OS Landranger 130 (Grantham): Explorer 248.
Path description: Village pavements, tracks, grass paths, arable land.
Start Point: West Road, Billingborough. NG34 0QD (GR 116343)
Parking: West Road, Billingborough; behind the fire station.
Dog friendly: Possibly off leads outside Billingborough village.
Public toilets: None; try Billingborough inns.
Nearest food: Billingborough; George & Dragon and Fortescue Arms.

BILLINGBOROUGH WALK

1. From the car park a passageway leads into the main street; there turn right. Once out of Billingborough continue for a quarter of a mile to a footpath sign on the right (by house number 78).

2. Walk up the gravel drive, go through a white gate and a smallholding to a second gate and then ahead on a track. When this bends right cross a footbridge, continuing along a grass path with first a ditch and then a hedge on your right. When the hedge ends bear slightly left to another footbridge in line with Sempringham church reaching the churchyard corner at a three-way footpath sign.

Approaching Sempringham

2A. The short route turns right here and the longer one goes left. Whichever route walkers choose they might first like to explore the churchyard with its memorial to St Gilbert and its Holy Well before walking down the approach track to visit the Princess Gwenllian memorial. For both routes walkers need to return to the churchyard.

3. [SHORT ROUTE] Go back to the footpath sign and continue along a grass path to a footbridge, then aim towards the left-hand end of a copse ahead and another bridge over a dyke. Head uphill aiming left of some trees peeping over the skyline; then pass to the left of a barn to meet a lane. [Rejoin the longer route here by turning right; see (*) below.]

4. [LONGER ROUTE] Walk through the churchyard and beyond the porch bear left to stile in a wall and join a fenced path between grass fields. At a grass track turn right for 300 yards to reach a signpost where a tree-lined lane (known as Primrose Lane) begins on the right. Follow this to a road and turn right following it into Birthorpe. Keep ahead through the village.

5. (*) At a fork in the road bear left. At a left-hand bend take the grass path ahead towards Billingborough church, continuing beside several field edges and eventually briefly cutting across the end of an arable field. At the next field

Holy Well

Princess Gwenllian Memorial

WALKS FOR ALL AGES - LINCOLNSHIRE

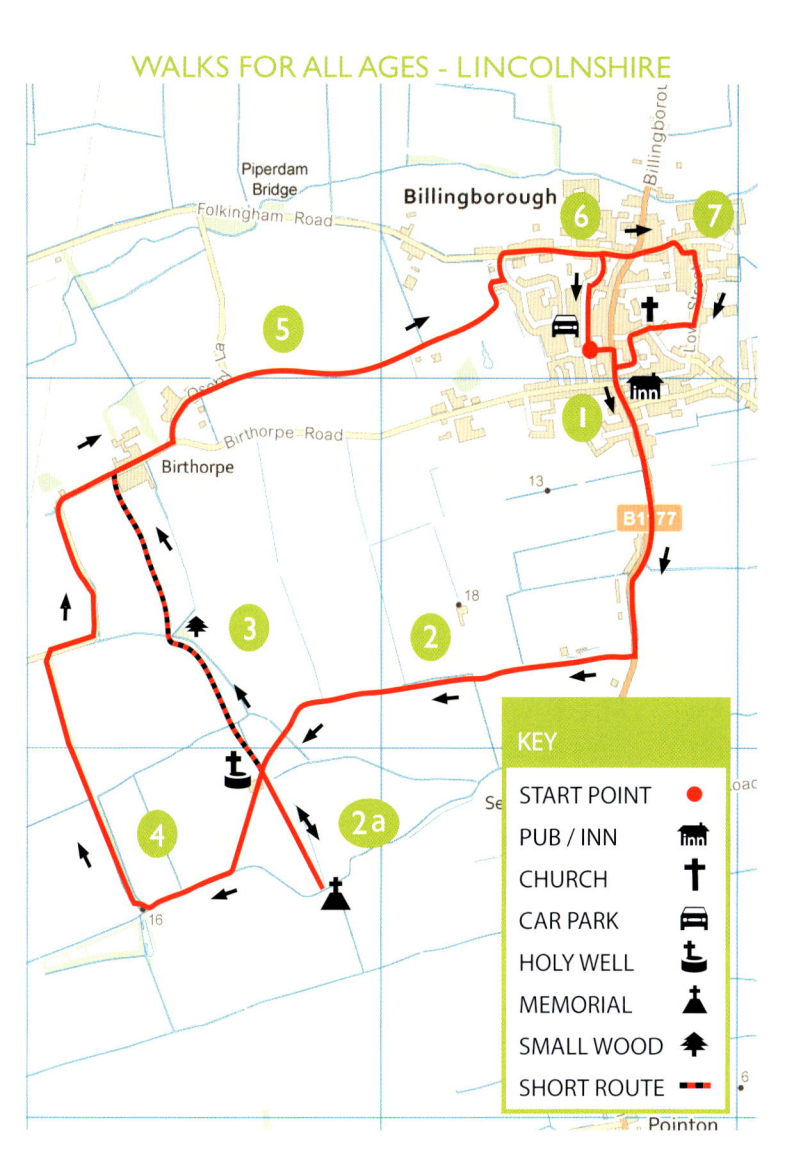

corner go left 35 yards then turn right, passing through a walled path between some new houses.

6. At the road go left and then right at the "T" junction. Back in Billingborough, at West Road – beyond the old station – turn right back to the car park.

7. However, to explore Billingborough keep ahead over the nearby crossroads into Vine Street. Turn right at Church Street and immediately cross into the walled passage opposite; then at the next road turn right. At Church Farm go right again along the path into the churchyard, staying left of the church and walking round the tower to join a lane. Go left past the millennium sundial then left again past the village pond and springs. At the next road go right and at the main street right again.

BISCATHORPE

This lovely walk explores the remote Wolds valleys of Biscathorpe and Gayton-le-Wold in beautiful yet contrasting scenery.

Extraordinary as it may seem some parts of the Lincolnshire Wolds have fewer inhabitants today than a thousand years ago. Two villages typifying this, both now almost disappeared, are Gayton-le-Wold and Biscathorpe.

The Wolds near Gayton

Biscathorpe is dominated by the massive Belmont TV mast standing to the south-west. This was built in 1965 and at 1,265 feet high was for several years England's tallest structure until it was shortened in preparation for digital transmission in 2010.

About halfway round the walk as we near Gayton-le-Wold, we pass Grange Farm, close to the site of Southorpe, yet another "lost" mediaeval village, which from about 1155 belonged to Kirkstead Abbey.

St Peter's Church

The Old English name Gayton-le-Wold means the "farmstead of the goats" but this area has been occupied since at least the Bronze Age (2,000 years BC). The evidence for this, however, is only visible nowadays from the air in the form of crop marks. There is one exception: Grim's Mound, a burial earthwork a short distance (and off our walk route) to the north-west at GR233869. In Anglo-Saxon times Gayton was the centre of a "Soke", that is a place authorized to hold a court, to impose and receive payment of fines. Saxon grave markers have been found near the tiny St Peter's church. This was rebuilt in 1889 and inside is displayed an old list of fees dating back to the days when weddings and funerals cost five shillings! (There's one in St Helen's at Biscathorpe too!)

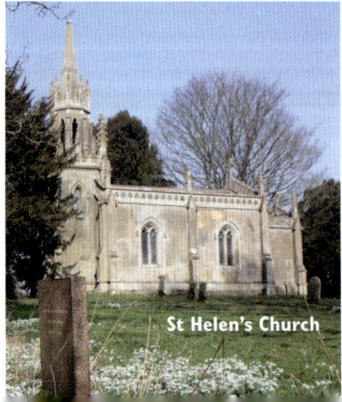

Lost Village

St Helen's Church

WALKS FOR ALL AGES - LINCOLNSHIRE

We finish the walk along a section of the Viking Way, and as we do so we get a bird's-eye view of Biscathorpe's picturesque St Helen's church, which is otherwise obscured by trees until one is close up to it. The descent also passes over the site of Biscathorpe mediaeval village, where earthworks and field outlines remain visible.

Nowadays only the church and one boarded-up house survive as isolated remnants of a place that had sixty-nine parishioners as recently as 1856. St Helen's was built in the 1830s and boasts a mass of pseudo-Gothic pinnacles. And curiously, the churchyard is within a ha-ha (a ditch) to keep out the cattle that graze on the surrounding grassland. Nearby are two fords where the River Bain, the Wolds' longest river, merges with the Gayton Beck.

NOTE. Biscathorpe lies north of Donington-on-Bain or can be reached southwards from the A157. A gated road leads to the church, the fords and ample roadside parking. It's an excellent picnic spot!

River Bain at Biscathorpe

THE BASICS

Distance in miles & km: 3½ miles: 5.5 kilometres.
Gradient: Several ascents and descents; none severe.
Severity: Moderate.
Approx time to walk: 120 mins.
Stiles: 8.
Maps: OS Landranger 122 (Skegness): Explorer 282.
Path description: Lanes, tracks, meadows and some arable land.
Start Point: Biscathorpe church. LN11 9RA approx. (GR 230849)
Parking: Plentiful parking space on open ground at Biscathorpe.
Dog friendly: Best on leads for most of the walk - cattle in fields.
Public toilets: None.
Nearest food: Black Horse, Donington-on-Bain.

BISCATHORPE WALK

1. With your back to Biscathorpe church turn right along the road and cross the footbridges at the two fords. The road then begins to climb and after about a quarter of a mile, as it swings gently left, take the track to the right. After another quarter of a mile branch right again along the hilltop until you reach a footpath signpost pointing left.

2. Turn here, walking out over the field for about 200 yards until Grange Farm comes into view a little to your left down in the valley ahead. Now bear half left towards the farm to locate a stile in a hedge. From this head directly across a rough meadow, keeping well left of the farm itself (and possibly detouring round a hollow that can be boggy after wet weather) to another stile seen in the far hedge on the skyline. Cross a farm track and keep ahead over an arable field. From another stile and waymark in the next hedge veer slightly right, gradually descending a long meadow to two more stiles at a footbridge in the right-hand fence. Cross these and turn left aiming towards a distant fence near the right-hand end of which is a stile by a field gate. Keep forward, close beside a fence to another stile at a lane.

3. Turn left towards Gayton-le-Wold and after approximately 300 yards climb the stile on the right just before the first house. (The church is a further 150 yards ahead!) From the stile head to a nearby footbridge, cross it and turn right along a track that soon starts curving to the left. Soon after, when the track bends right, leave it heading towards the footbridge seen a few yards away. Cross it, and bear half left past a small shed and then proceed diagonally across a large, arable field heading towards its top right-hand corner where a kissing gate accesses a grass track. Now turn right up to a road where you join the Viking Way!

WALKS FOR ALL AGES - LINCOLNSHIRE

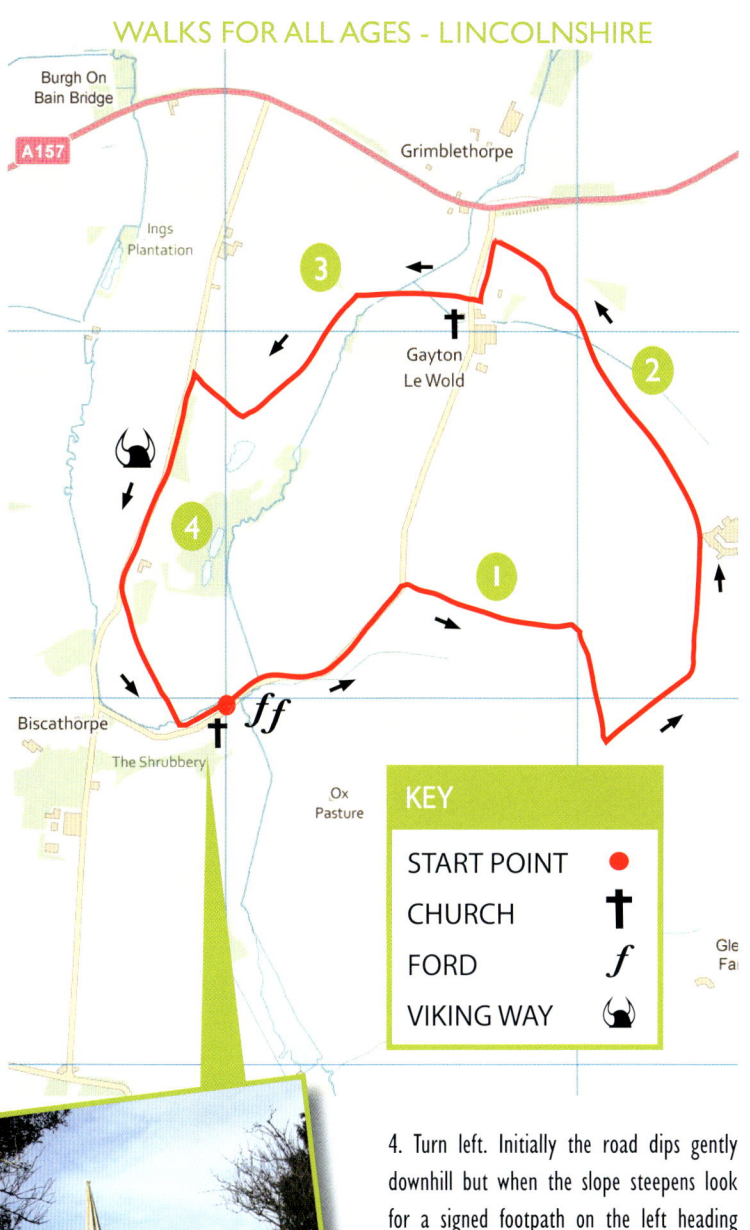

KEY

START POINT ●
CHURCH ✝
FORD *f*
VIKING WAY

4. Turn left. Initially the road dips gently downhill but when the slope steepens look for a signed footpath on the left heading into some woods. From a kissing gate continue downhill across Biscathorpe "lost" village to a footbridge over the River Bain near the church.

BOSTON TO ANTON'S GOWT

This "there-and-back" walk follows the River Witham between Boston and Anton's Gowt. It is almost entirely along the Water Rail Way, a long-distance walking/cycle route along a former railway that links Boston with Lincoln.

Until 250 years ago the River Witham upstream from Boston was tidal as far inland as Chapel Hill. Shifting channels and silting had constantly made navigation difficult and as far back as the 16th century, the time of Elizabeth I, plans to remedy the situation achieved nothing. When drainage schemes were finally undertaken in the 1630s under Charles I, their primary aim was improving fenland drainage rather than navigation along the river.

The River Withams

However in 1743/44 two famous drainage engineers, John Grundy of Spalding and his son (another John) surveyed the area to ascertain what could be done to improve the Witham's winding course. But their recommendations were deemed too costly and again nothing was done until 1761 when John Grundy (Junior) and eminent civil engineer John Smeaton resurrected the earlier plans with new estimates of £54,000. By June 1762 an Act of Parliament had given the go-ahead to build the Grand Sluice at Boston and straighten the river up to Chapel Hill. That work, completed by 1766, resulted in the Witham looking much as it does today.

To Anton's Gowt

The Great Northern Railway's Lincolnshire "Loop Line" opened in 1848 as the main line from London (via Peterborough and Boston) to the north and it closely followed the Witham between Boston and Lincoln. Within four years, however, its importance was considerably lessened when the more direct "Towns Line" through Grantham was opened. Even so, traffic on the "Loop Line" declined only gradually with the first stations closing in 1940, and both passenger and goods services surviving until 1970.

The Hall Hills creosoting works was purchased in the 1880s by the GNR to pressure treat timber, imported through Boston from the Baltic, for their

Grand Sluice Boston

WALKS FOR ALL AGES - LINCOLNSHIRE

railway sleepers. Hall Hills closed in 1965 but the buildings can still be seen from the footpath near the walk's halfway point. As we approach Anton's Gowt we see (and who can resist climbing it?) the new Boston Pendulum, a futuristic viewing platform designed by Dutch architect Paul Robbrecht.

The name Anton's Gowt commemorates Sir Anthony Thomas, a notable drainage engineer of the 1630s. His work included early schemes to drain the East Fen and he is believed to have also cut Boston's Maud Foster Drain. Anton's Gowt lock, which measures 72 feet long, can accommodate boats with a draught of 3 feet, and gives access to the Frith Bank Drain and, via another lock at Cowbridge, to the system of waterways known as the Witham Navigable Drains. These total some 40 miles, although actual navigation is nowadays somewhat theoretical in places. There are information boards by the lock-keeper's cottage.

On arrival at Anton's Gowt walkers can recuperate at the Malcolm Arms before retracing their steps to Boston.

The View from Pendulum Tower

THE BASICS

Distance in miles & km: 5 miles: 8 kilometres.
Gradient: Level pedestrian and cycleway throughout.
Severity: Easy.
Approx time to walk: 140 mins.
Stiles: None.
Maps: OS Landranger 131 (Boston): Explorer 261.
Path description: Level surfaced path virtually throughout.
Start Point: Grand Sluice, Boston. PE21 9JU (GR 300475)
Parking: Ltd at Sluice Bridge. "Pay & Display" in Tunnard Street.
Dog friendly: Best on leads.
Public toilets: Only at inns.
Nearest food: Witham Tavern. The Jolly Sailors Café. Malcolm Arms.

BOSTON - ANTON'S GOWT WALK

The inn is named after the Malcolm family, former local landowners, one of whom became Boston's MP during the 1860's. (From Anton's Gowt the riverside path continues towards Langrick for those wishing to extend the walk.)

The route also passes the 39-acre Witham Country Park (worth a possible detour), created by Boston Borough Council partly with European Union grants.

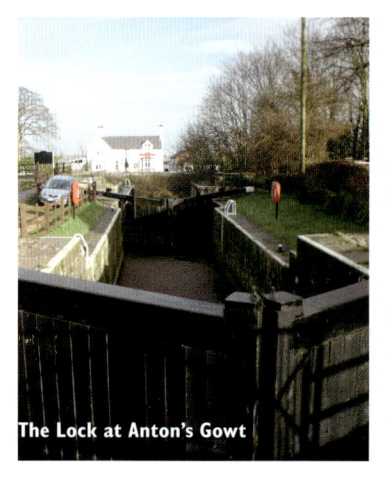

The Lock at Anton's Gowt

The return walk has fine views of the famous "Stump" for much of the way. Another bonus is an inn and café near the Grand Sluice back in Boston!
NOTE. Alternatively do the walk in reverse from Anton's Gowt. The postcode is PE22 7BE (GR 531475).

Returning to Boston

1. Walk under the railway bridge and past the Witham Tavern to pick up the riverside path out into the countryside and join the surfaced Water Rail Way.

The Walk Starts Here

2. Continue on this, although in places it is possible to walk on grass closer to the river. After a mile or so, when a footpath joins from the right near Hall Hills, stay by the river.

3. Keep ahead, past the Boston Pendulum until the white-painted lock-keeper's cottage at Anton's Gowt appears ahead some 400 yards away. Here another footpath joins from the right; take this. Walk down to the Frith Bank Drain and cross the bridge to a road. Now turn left for the Malcolm Arms.

Near to Grand Sluice

WALKS FOR ALL AGES - LINCOLNSHIRE

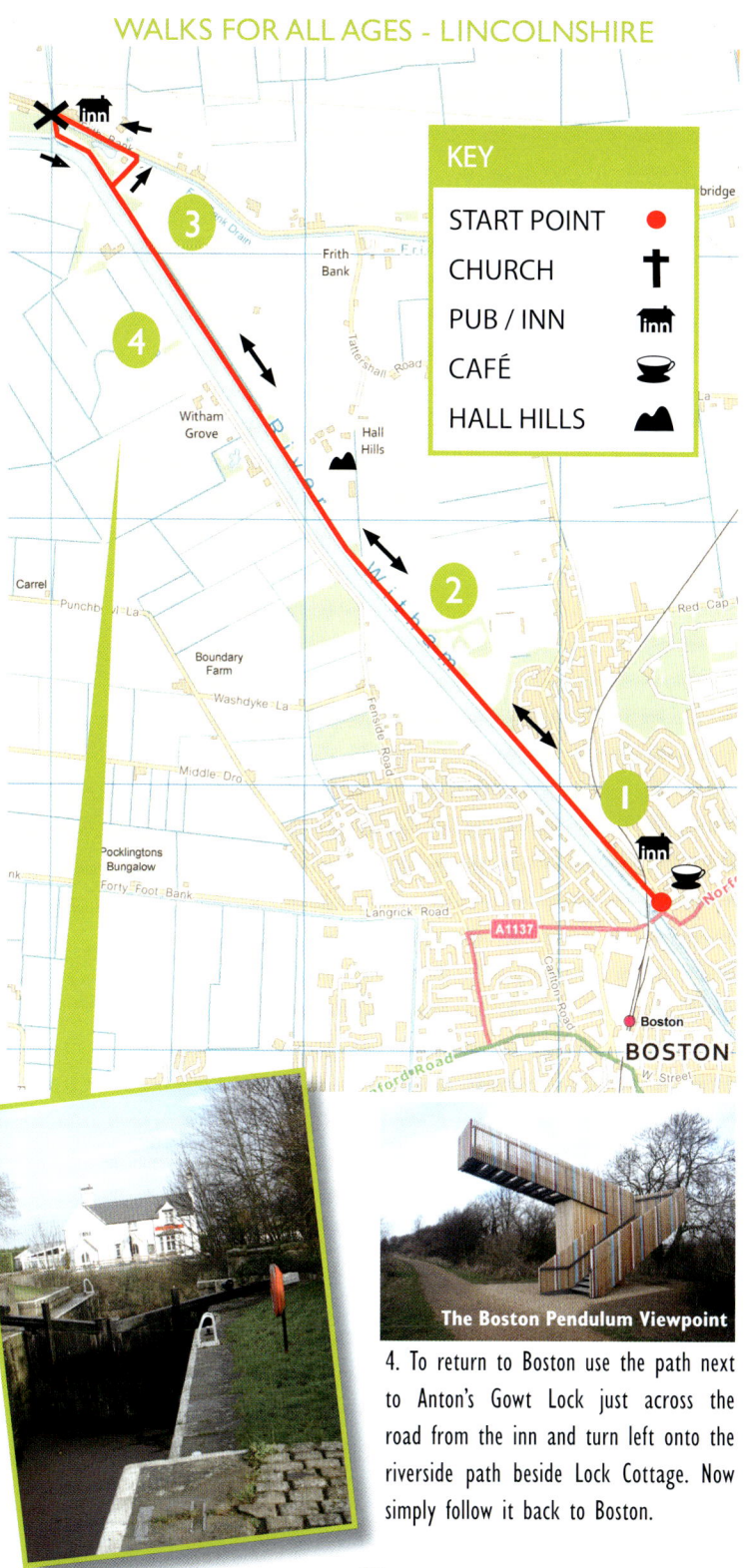

KEY

- START POINT — ●
- CHURCH — †
- PUB / INN — 🏠
- CAFÉ — ☕
- HALL HILLS — ⛰

The Boston Pendulum Viewpoint

4. To return to Boston use the path next to Anton's Gowt Lock just across the road from the inn and turn left onto the riverside path beside Lock Cottage. Now simply follow it back to Boston.

CULVERTHORPE

This route is ideal for any time of year but with no arable land to cross is particularly suited to an autumn or winter outing.

The walk begins from the North Kesteven District Council's Culverthorpe "Stepping Out" car park and explores the environs of Culverthorpe Hall using both public rights of way and some of NKDC's "Stepping Out" footpath network.

The Hall and its park epitomises the archetypal English country house; a grand façade, its own "Park" farm, landscaped grounds, lakes, mature trees and extensive vistas.

Culverthorpe Lake

Culverthorpe village was probably bigger in 1086 than it is today since the Domesday Book informs us that it then comprised three carucates of taxable land — a carucate was a vague measurement that could vary between 120 and 200 of our modern acres — farmed by eight villagers and that there was a church and a priest. If there really was a church it has now long disappeared and the reference may be to nearby Heydour, since no trace of a mediaeval church has ever been found.

Culverthorpe Park

The hall is partly 17th century and partly 18th century and was begun about 1680 by Sir John Newton, a cousin of Sir Isaac Newton, and Member of Parliament for Grantham. Sir John's house comprised what is today's central section and has been described as having "the air of a French chateau". The original house was extended when side wings were added by Sir John's descendent Sir Michael about 1730, probably for reasons of status as he had married into another Newton baronetcy (though of an unrelated family) and his new wife was Margaret, Countess Coningsby. However their lives were not without tragedy for in 1733, when their baby son was only three months old, he was killed when a pet monkey threw him over the balcony of their London home. During World War II the hall was used as a forces billet but has since become a private home again.

Culverthorpe Lake Vista

In spite of the remarks above about Culverthorpe having no parish church a private chapel to the hall was built in about 1691. Although later

WALKS FOR ALL AGES - LINCOLNSHIRE

demolished the frontage with its Ionic columns was saved and re-erected amongst the trees to the east of the hall beside the lane leading towards Wilsford and Rauceby. Seeing it requires a short detour and this is best done during late autumn or winter when the trees have no leaves. (See section 4 (*) in the route guide below.)

The longer walk has fine views across rolling countryside to Sleaford and beyond.

NOTES. Culverthorpe lies to the north of the A52 and can be reached by turning off through Dembleby.

Culverthorpe Lake in Spring

The Chapel in the Woods

THE BASICS

Distance in miles & km: ¾ or 4½ miles: 1.5 or 7 kilometres.
Gradient: Gentle, easy ascents / descents only.
Severity: Easy.
Approx time to walk: 30 mins (short) or 120 mins (longer).
Stiles: Short route 1; Long route 3.
Maps: OS Landranger 130 (Grantham): Explorer 248.
Path description: Grass paths, farm tracks and country lanes.
Start Point: Culverthorpe "Stepping Out" car park. (GR 019399)
Parking: At start.
Dog friendly: In parts — but on a lead in Culverthorpe park.
Public toilets: None.
Nearest food: The nearest inn is the Houblon Arms in Oasby.

CULVERTHORPE WALK

1. As you enter the car park look to your right for the start of a lakeside footpath. After about 300 yards this joins a road where you should turn left for a further 300 yards or so. (At this point a footpath on the left crosses the lake dam and at the far side links up with the main route; thus forming the short circular walk round the lake.)

Culverthorpe Lake (Springtime)

2. Just ahead, however, and on the right-hand side of the road, is another footpath sign pointing along a farm track. Follow this for about half a mile to join another quiet country lane and turn left. In a "short" mile another "Stepping Out" path goes off to the left.

3. This well-waymarked path makes two left-hand and two right-hand turns before following a field edge path down to footbridge in a valley. Just beyond that bear right up a short, hedged section then go left by a stream. On reaching a waymark cross over so that the stream is now to your right. Then walk to the road at Culverthorpe.

4. Turn right and head up into the village, going left at the first road junction and keeping ahead (past a "No Through Road" sign) through the magnificent gateway into the Hall's park.

Culverthorpe Hall Entrance

(*) (Note, however, the lane branching off to the right; 100 yards along this, and on the left, is the rebuilt chapel mentioned in the introduction.)

5. Continue into the park for 60 yards, then climb the stile on your left. Walk beside a fence to another stile and follow the fenced path almost to the lakeshore. At a waymarked path junction consider going a few yards ahead to savour the views across the lake; otherwise turn right along another fenced path, which has one stile.

WALKS FOR ALL AGES - LINCOLNSHIRE

KEY

- START POINT ●
- SHORT ROUTE ▬▬
- CHAPEL RUIN ᛭

6. At a kissing gate join an estate road and turn left across a causeway between two lakes. At the far side a short path through trees on the left leads into the car park.

31

FRAMPTON MARSH

The Frampton Marsh RSPB reserve opened in 2009 and this walk offers an interesting day out exploring local footpaths in addition to visiting the reserve and its three observation hides.

To start with the walk follows an old, inner sea bank. For centuries these earthworks have been vital to the fens as flood defences and some date back to the early Middle Ages. It was once thought that the Romans devised the first such banks but this seems unlikely, and those locally referred to as "Roman Banks" are certainly later in origin although their precise ages remain uncertain. Even the county archaeological records shed little light on this subject but their most likely date is usually accepted as mediaeval — and probably from the 14th century onwards. They were gradually added to over the centuries and were still the first line of defence until World War II when concrete pillboxes were built on them; we see one of these early in the walk.

Today's outer bank (obviously post-WWII) provides far-reaching 360-degree panoramic views stretching seawards over the Welland Outfall and across The Wash to the Holbeach bombing ranges as well as inland. The ranges opened in 1928 and are still used by the RAF and NATO. Before re-entering the reserve the walk includes views of Cut End and the embankments constraining the modern Witham Haven together with Boston "Stump", and the ancient marshland creeks to our right are the remnants of the River Witham's original course. This outer bank also forms an early section of the Macmillan Way, the long-distance trail from Boston to the Dorset coast. Seats provide strategic viewpoints as well as pleasant rest stops.

Our main reason for being at Frampton, of course, is the new RSPB reserve. This includes tracts of The Wash salt marshes owned by the RSPB since 1984 that form part of the largest National Nature Reserve in England. Inshore from the bank the RSPB's efforts represent the culmination of several years' work developing almost 400 acres of reed beds, freshwater lagoons and wet grassland. Each of these habitats has its own importance for different coastal and marshland birds, including the thousands of geese and wading birds that visit during migration or for winter refuge. All this is overlooked by three hides: the East Hide, the 360 Degree Hide and the Reedbed Hide. The visitor centre can provide a reserve map.

Across The Wash the RSPB has allowed the sea to penetrate part of its freshwater reserve at Titchwell in Norfolk and so Frampton, it is hoped, will compensate for this by attracting (amongst other species) one of Titchwell's most spectacular species, the avocet – the beautiful bird on the RSPB logo.

You will almost certainly see cattle in the new wetland meadows, on the marsh, and sometimes on the sea banks. Their presence here is essential since grazing helps create breeding habitats for birds such as redshanks.

The visitor centre has free parking and toilet facilities, visual displays about the reserve, a daily "sightings"

RSPB Reserve Water Meadows

THE BASICS

Distance in miles & km: 3 or 4½ miles: 5 or 7.5 kilometres.
Gradient: Mostly level.
Severity: Easy.
Approx time to walk: Up to 120 mins.
Stiles: None. Sea banks accessed by steps.
Maps: OS Landranger 131 (Boston): Explorer 249.
Path description: Grass and surfaced paths.
Start Point: Frampton Marsh RSPB visitor centre. PE20 1AY (GR358390)
Parking: Free at start.
Dog friendly: No, dogs not permitted on the reserve.
Public toilets: At RSPB visitor centre.
Nearest food: Drinks at visitor centre. Moores Arms, Frampton.

FRAMPTON MARSH WALK

board and telescopes for visitors' use. But if you have your own binoculars bring them to use during the walk and in the hides. The shorter three-mile route does not directly pass any reserve hides; the full route passes close to all three.

1. From the car park turn left back down the approach road for 100 yards before going left at a footpath sign and handgate along an old sea bank. This enclosed, tree-lined path is in complete contrast to the surrounding open marshland. Continue until the path meets a lane then turn left again for about 200 yards. When the lane bends left keep ahead through a gate along another bank to reach a WWII pillbox and footpath sign.

2. Turn left along another grass bank (Cross Bank) and at the outer sea bank climb steps to a kissing gate on the top. Walk forwards briefly and then follow the bank leftwards. In just under half a mile you will come to another kissing gate and more steps to your left. (These and the track below form the "short" route back to the visitor centre.)

3. The main route continues along the sea bank for another three-quarters of a mile, before swinging leftwards to reach access steps to the nature reserve.

On The Sea Bank

4. At the bottom initially bear right a few paces then take the first side path on the left for the East Hide. Return and keep left and at another path junction turn left again; you will then soon come to the Reedbed Hide followed by the short access path for the 360 Degree Hide.

5. Continue until the main path meets a lane and turn right back to the visitor centre.

WW2 Pillbox

RSPB Visitor Centre

WALKS FOR ALL AGES - LINCOLNSHIRE

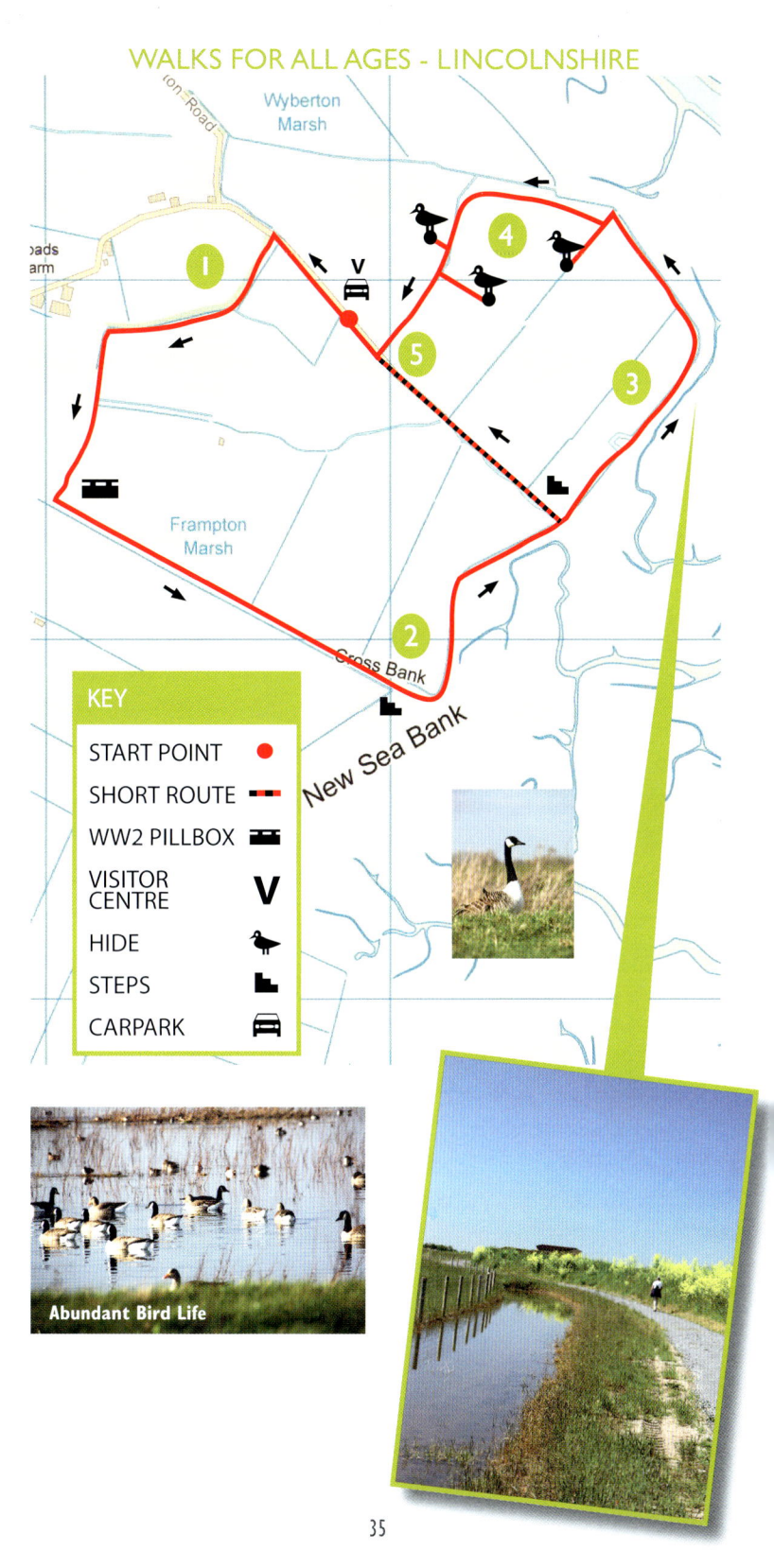

KEY

- START POINT ●
- SHORT ROUTE ▬
- WW2 PILLBOX
- VISITOR CENTRE V
- HIDE
- STEPS
- CARPARK

Abundant Bird Life

HAGWORTHINGHAM

A great destination in the southern Wolds is the Snipe Dales Country Park and Nature Reserve. Our visit, however, starts from the neighbouring village of Hagworthingham.

The walk is perhaps the most strenuous in this book but there is compensation in the unusual experience of twice crossing the Greenwich Meridian line at GR's 336692 and 336687.

Holy Trinity Church at Hagworthingham dates mainly from the late 12th century. In the north wall, near the chancel arch, is a little plain, glass window that may have been to allow lepers to watch services from outside. The tower collapsed in 1972.

Meridian Marker

Visible just off route before we enter the nature reserve is a stone circle placed there by the landowner and based (I'm told) upon Chakra, the Hindu concept of wheel-like centres of energy.

Holy Trinity Church

The combined Snipe Dales Country Park and Nature Reserve covers 220 acres with the nature reserve occupying the western end of the Winceby Beck valley and the Country Park the eastern end; they are jointly managed by Lincolnshire County Council and Lincolnshire Wildlife Trust. Their importance derives from their geology. The beck has cut down through overlying sandstone beds to the clay beneath, thus creating a marshy environment in the valley floor but drier slopes above; this gives a wide variety of habitats.

One intriguing feature is a water ram where an information board explains how water pressure can be made to push more water uphill. The system was invented in 1796 by the Frenchman Joseph Montgolfier who was, with his brother Jacques, a famous pioneer of hot-air balloons.

The Climb to Winceby Church

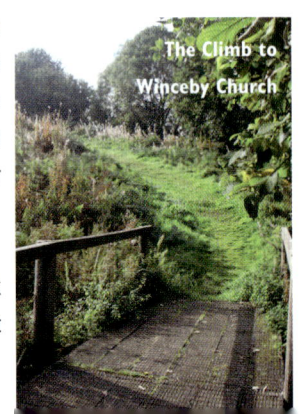

Winceby was recorded in the Domesday Book (1086) as "Winzebi" and its last church was built in 1860 and demolished in 1964; now only a few gravestones remain in the abandoned churchyard.

The Civil War Battle of Winceby was fought on 11th October 1643. The Parliamentarians under Oliver Cromwell met an advancing Royalist force roughly where Winceby House now stands. The Royalists only briefly withstood Cromwell's pre-emptive charge before fleeing, only to be blocked by the dense Winceby/Scrafield parish hedge where the only gate opened towards them. Once the Parliamentarians caught up a massacre ensued and contemporary accounts say the blood ran ankle deep in what has since been known as "Slash Hollow" (GR 312686). The Victorian Winceby House has a memorial carved from a piece of Louth station platform on its front lawn.

Near Winceby House

THE BASICS

Distance: 5¼ miles: 8.5 kilometres.
Gradient: The route includes some short, steep sections.
Severity: Moderate, Hilly with numerous stiles.
Approx time to walk: 180 mins.
Stiles: 12.
Maps: OS Landranger 122 (Skegness): Explorer 273.
Path description: Fields, grassy paths, and surfaced paths.
Start Point: The George & Dragon. PE23 4NA (GR 346696)
Parking: At the inn.
Dog friendly: Yes but on leads in the reserve and park.
Public toilets: At the country park, or at the inn.
Nearest food: Hagworthingham: the George and Dragon inn.

HAGWORTHINGHAM MAP

1. Leave the inn car park, turn right and then go left down Church Lane. Just beyond Holy Trinity church take the gated path on the right by Woodside Cottage.

2. From a second gate proceed past a barn, then through a metal bridle gate and along a fenced path to a stile.

3. Keep ahead gently uphill to a hedge gap and then on to a prominent hedge end and waymark post. Join a track and keep forward until this does a hairpin bend. Cut the corner through some trees – passing a footpath sign and simultaneously crossing the Greenwich meridian! On rejoining the track go left

WALKS FOR ALL AGES - LINCOLNSHIRE

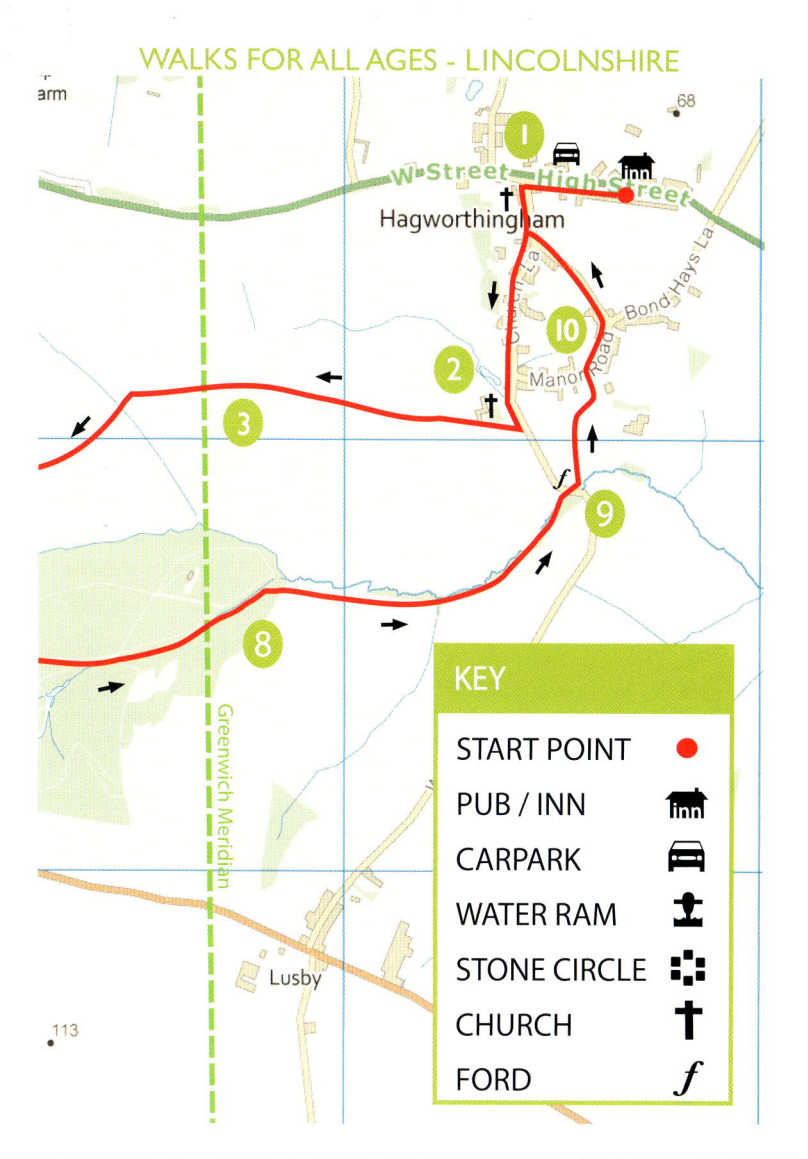

KEY

- START POINT ●
- PUB / INN
- CARPARK
- WATER RAM
- STONE CIRCLE
- CHURCH †
- FORD *f*

down to a footbridge and then uphill to a fingerpost in a hedge gap on the skyline. (The stone circle is visible here.)

4. Once through the hedge, contour around a hollow on a faint track, then veer left to reach a bridlegate and go steeply downhill to enter Snipe Dales Nature Reserve at a stile and footbridge.

5. At the first path junction turn right along a broad path heading up the valley. Beyond the water ram, at a hilltop, reach a gate and a footbridge before climbing

HAGWORTHINGHAM WALK

steeply (there's a seat halfway up!) into Winceby's old churchyard.

6. Climb the stile by the access gate and immediately turn left to another stile, then cross a paddock, keeping to the right of a chicken shed. From another stile turn right through a farmyard to the road. Turn left and immediately after Winceby House climb the stile on the left. Cross the large meadow diagonally aiming for a footpath sign and stile seen near trees at the far side.

7. Re-enter the nature reserve and follow a downhill path beside a fence to a stile and bridlegate. At the second yellow arrow waymark ignore a footbridge, instead turning right to follow a steep path into some hilltop trees and leave the nature reserve to enter the country park.

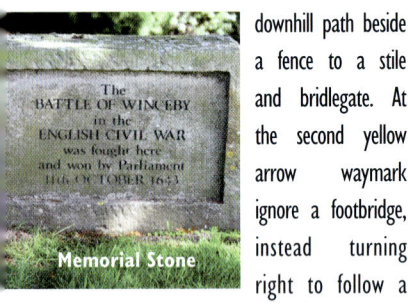

Memorial Stone

8. Bear right and at a path junction go left along a hilltop track and, ignoring side paths and tracks, keep ahead whilst going gradually downhill. After re-crossing the meridian line you will come to a fingerpost reading "Footpath to Hagworthingham". Climb the nearby stile and follow a well-trodden path along the lower edge of a hilly meadow. From a kissing gate continue by a fence to the road near Hagworthingham ford.

9. Cross the road, climb the stile opposite and almost immediately go left over a footbridge. Walk uphill, climbing two more stiles that lead to a fenced path, another stile and a house drive. Go left to the public road.

Snipe Dales

10. Turn right and then take the first left back into Hagworthingham village and the start.

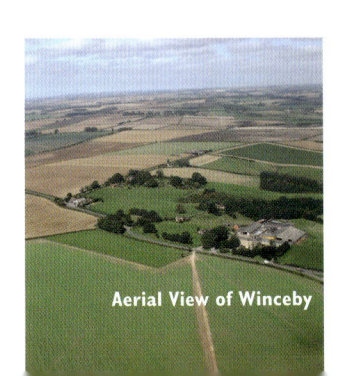

Winceby House

Aerial View of Winceby

Hagworthingham Church

HAXEY

The Isle of Axholme is an under-appreciated walking area even though it has numerous well-marked footpaths. This short walk gives a taste of its varied scenery.

This may well be an area of Lincolnshire new to many readers. The route offers a considerable variety of scenery including deep, secluded railway cuttings as well as the open Axholme "moors" backed by the hills of the "Isle of Axholme".

A little history first! Haxey's name is of Scandinavian origin and means "Haki's Island", so it is an ancient settlement. However, following a devastating fire in 1741 little remained apart from the church. St Nicholas's has early Norman stonework inside whilst the exterior is mainly 15th century, though with inevitable Victorian restoration. Near the eastern wall of the

Church Street Haxey

churchyard is the stump of a market cross used as the "Fool's" stone during the annual Haxey Hood game (of which more below), while at the north-west corner an extraordinary lytchgate revolves around a central post.

The surrounding low-lying area was once peat bog, over which the local villages exercised rights to cut peat and turves. Drainage was begun in the 1620s at the request of King Charles I, in order to create more profitable agricultural land, and the work was undertaken by Cornelius Vermuyden, the famous Dutch engineer. He met with considerable, often violent, opposition from the local people, who saw the scheme as a threat to their way of life and feared for the loss of their valuable rights.

At its far end Church Street becomes Greenhill, where another market cross carries the emblem of a white lion on a red shield. These are the arms of the Mowbray family, who in the mediaeval times were the Lords of Epworth Manor, which included Haxey and Westwoodside.

Mowbray Cross

Haxey is of course celebrated for its annual "Hood Game" played on 6th January – being Epiphany and the "twelfth day" of Christmas. The "game" involves teams from Haxey and Westwoodside battling vigorously to secure a leather "hood" and return it to their local inn. The game's origins

WALKS FOR ALL AGES - LINCOLNSHIRE

date from around the 13th century and supposedly recall the occasion on a windy, winter's day when Lady Mowbray was out riding and lost her scarf (hood) in the wind. One of a group of farm labourers nearby rushed to rescue it but was too nervous to return it personally. Another, who did so, Lady Mowbray dubbed a "Lord" — and the former a "Fool" — but then donated land to them all, provided they re-enacted the incident each year.

The walk also follows part of the abandoned Isle of Axholme Joint Railway. Authorised by Parliament in 1898 it was the first line ever built under the 1896 Light Railways Act, passed to encourage the construction of inexpensive rural lines without incurring costly Parliamentary legal fees. It opened in January 1905 but passenger trains had ceased by 1933, though goods services survived until 1965.

Westwoodside's name has a literal meaning for the village developed near woodland on the west edge of the Mowbray estates. It became a stronghold of Methodism under John Wesley, who was born at nearby Epworth, and who often preached there. Westwoodside once had three chapels, and a survivor stands in Nethergate on the route of our walk.

THE BASICS

Distance in miles & km: 5½ miles: 9 kilometres.
Gradient: Almost flat.
Severity: Easy, some ups and downs.
Approx time to walk: 120 mins.
Stiles: None.
Maps: OS Landranger 112 (Scunthorpe): Explorer 280.
Path description: Village pavements, old railway, open countryside.
Start Point: Haxey church. DN9 2HY (GR 765998)
Parking: Church Street, Haxey.
Dog friendly: Best off-lead section is on old railway.
Public toilets: Only at inns.
Nearest food: The Duke William & The Loco inns. The Carpenters Arms.

HAXEY WALK

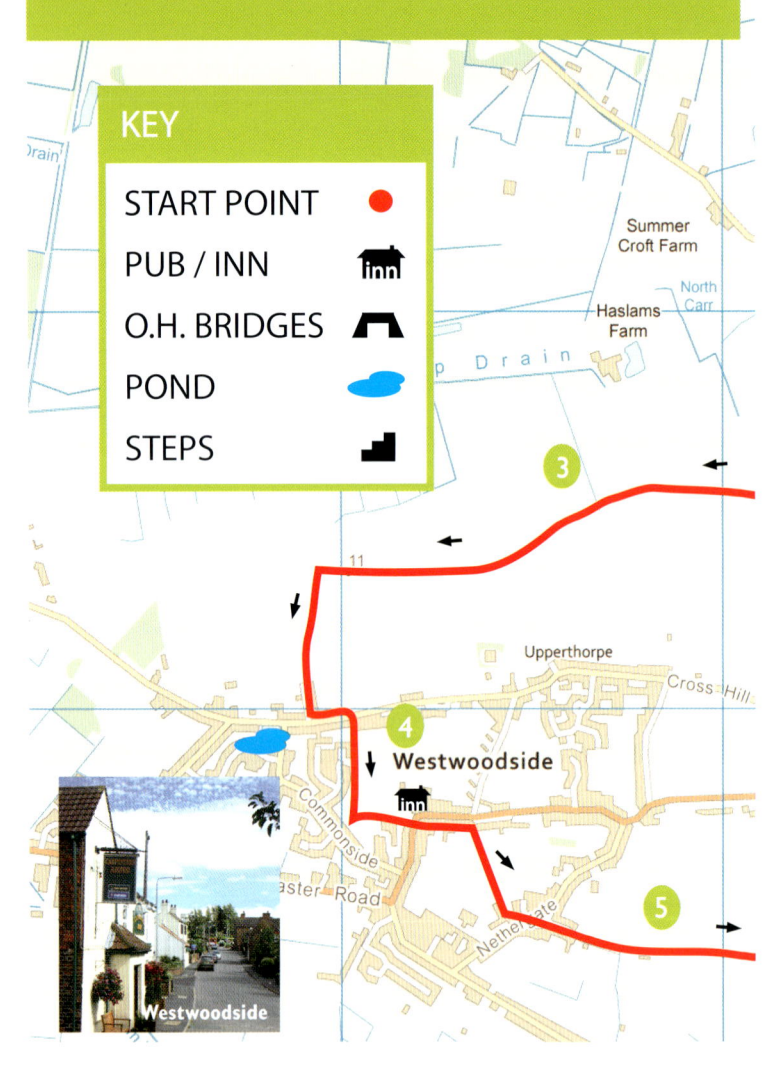

KEY
- START POINT ●
- PUB / INN
- O.H. BRIDGES
- POND
- STEPS

Westwoodside

1. Begin by heading away from the church and at Green Hill bear right down High Street past the Post Office. After Marlborough Avenue (and just before the 1909 chapel) look for a gate on the left giving access to the old railway.

2. Walk along this to a ramp by the school. Cross the road and descend a corresponding ramp opposite by an information board. Now continue along the trackbed, passing under two overhead bridges. Once the cutting becomes an embankment, descend left down steps beside the brick parapet of an under-bridge to join a grass track.

3. Keep ahead for three-quarters of a mile to a surfaced road. Turn left for a few yards only and then veer right on a grassy, rising path between animal paddocks. At the top (near a farm) turn right along another track for approximately a mile

WALKS FOR ALL AGES - LINCOLNSHIRE

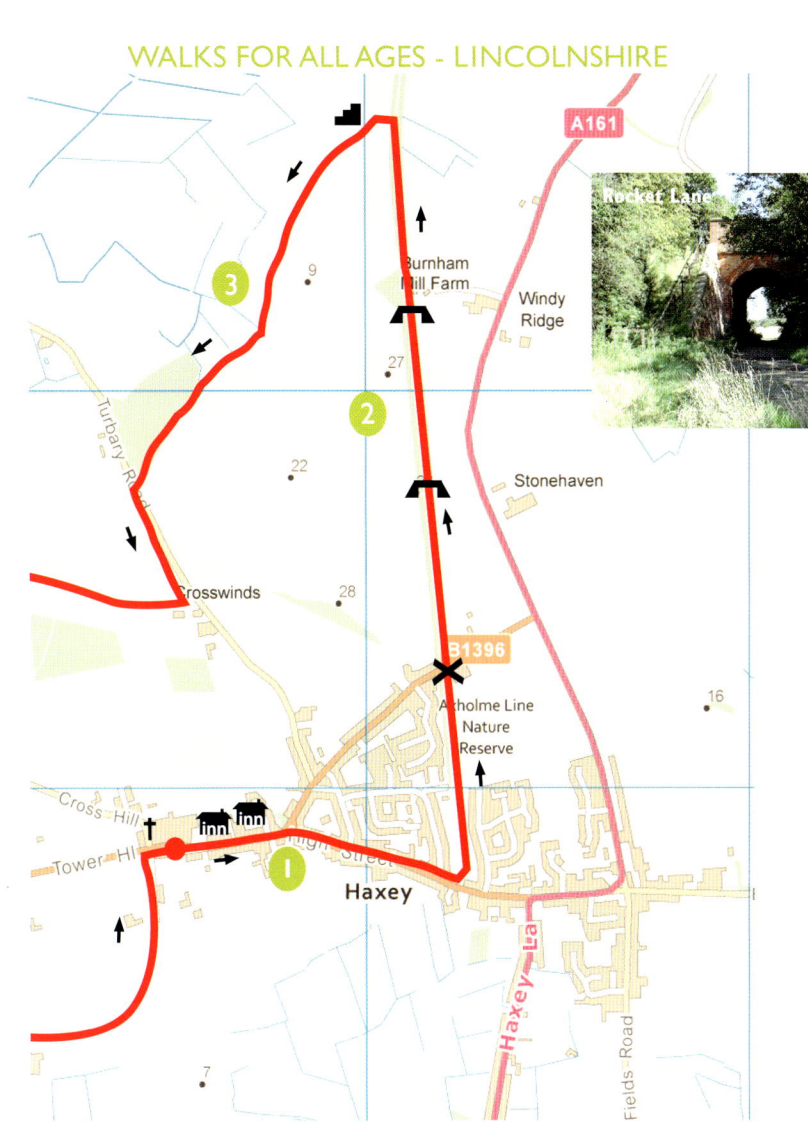

until the hillside to your left falls away and the houses of Westwoodside appear. Now take a track branching left, which soon becomes a lane before meeting the road of Upperthorpe Hill. (A short detour to the right visits Westwoodside pond – then return.)

4. Otherwise turn left and after 150 yards go right at a signed footpath between houses. At a path junction bear left to the Carpenters Arms in Westwoodside. Keep forward up the road (Brethergate) for 200 yards and then turn right along the footpath opposite the end of Gollands Lane.

5. At another road (Nethergate) cross into Sandbeds Lane and after about 100 yards veer right at a junction to continue along a grassy track. This soon bears gently leftwards heading up to Haxey churchyard. Climb some large stone steps and walk through the churchyard back into Church Street.

45

HEIGHINGTON & BRANSTON

Heighington and Branston are two stone-built villages to the southeast of Lincoln. At Branston we discover a link to King George III and a secret waterwheel.

In recent years Heighington has seen many new houses built, but the village centre retains its pleasing mixture of stone and brick buildings. The Post Office, covered with bright green tiles, is quite unusual. St Thomas's Church is concealed behind a wall and its churchyard was surfaced to make a playground when it served as the school from 1865 until quite recently.

Some Norman masonry remains from the mediaeval church that had become ruinous by 1619 when Thomas Garrett, a local landowner, restored it as a chapel; Heighington's "Heritage Room" is named after him. The tower clock was paid for by public subscription in 1924 to commemorate villagers who served in the Great War.

At Branston, All Saints Church blends architectural styles from the Saxons to the 1960s. On Christmas Day 1962 the chancel was gutted by fire but it was rebuilt by 1966, although in a modern style that Nikolaus Pevsner, the architectural historian, describes as "unhappily at odds" with the old church; though the villagers no doubt disagree! In the car park opposite look for Branston's history mosaic, one panel of which dramatically depicts the fire.

Nearby is the Georgian Rectory built in 1765 by Peregrine Curtois, one of a family that provided the rectors here continuously for 211 years between 1680 and 1891. The Curtois family also provides our link with "Mad" King George III. One of the king's doctors, who was almost single-handedly responsible for his recovery from what is now considered to have been porphyria, was a Dr Francis Willis, who married a daughter of Branston's Reverend John Curtois in 1749. The former Bertie Arms nearby in Hall Lane bears a plaque recording the 1765 meetings there of the Enclosures Commissioners.

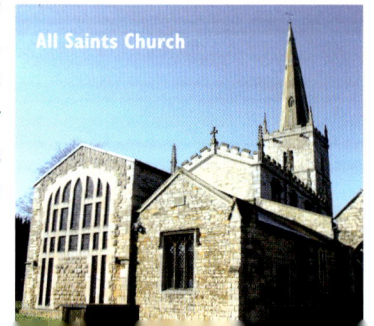

WALKS FOR ALL AGES - LINCOLNSHIRE

Around Branston too you will see numerous artworks and plaques that form a village trail. (Guides are usually obtainable at the café.)

We also visit Branston's restored village waterwheel – in Waterwheel Lane, of course! Installed in 1879 it supplied Branston Hall and houses of other local gentry until the village had mains water installed in the 1960s.

We return to Heighington across the high ground of Washingborough Top, where extensive views include Lincoln and the cathedral.

A shorter route, omitting Branston, is described in the route instructions.

Hall Lane - Branston

THE BASICS

Distance in miles & km: 3 or 6½ miles: 5 or 10.5 kilometres.
Gradient: Generally easy; one longish, gradual climb in section 6.
Severity: Easy.
Approx time to walk: 75 mins or 180 mins.
Stiles: None.
Maps: OS Landranger 121 (Lincoln): Explorer 272.
Path description: Village pavements, country roads, farm tracks and meadows.
Start Point: Heighington; car park access: Mill Lane. (GR 030694)
Parking: At start.
Dog friendly: Only in parts.
Public toilets: None.
Nearest food: Turk's Head, Food for Thought Coffee Shop, Waggon & Horses.

HEIGHINGTON & BRANSTON MAP

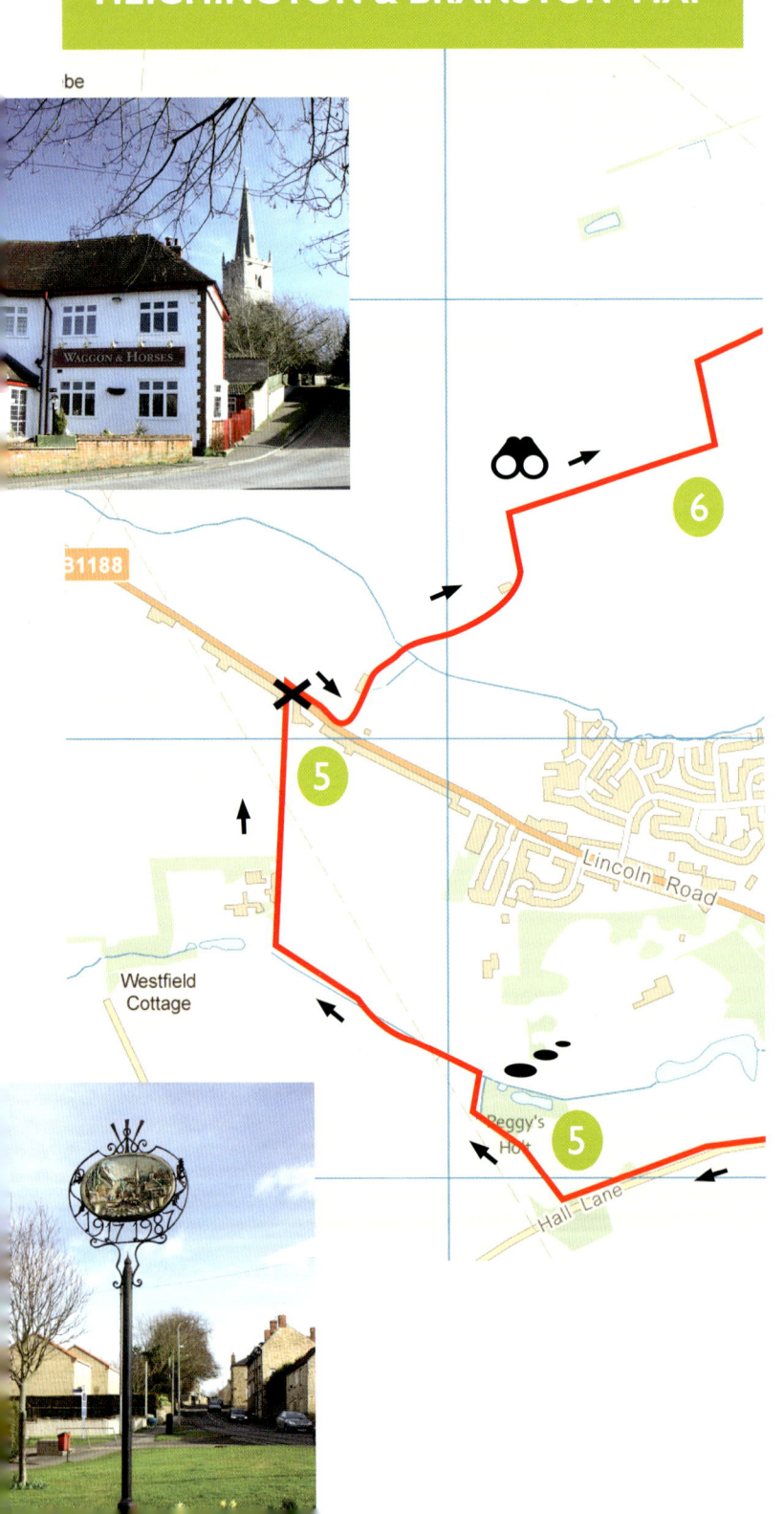

WALKS FOR ALL AGES - LINCOLNSHIRE

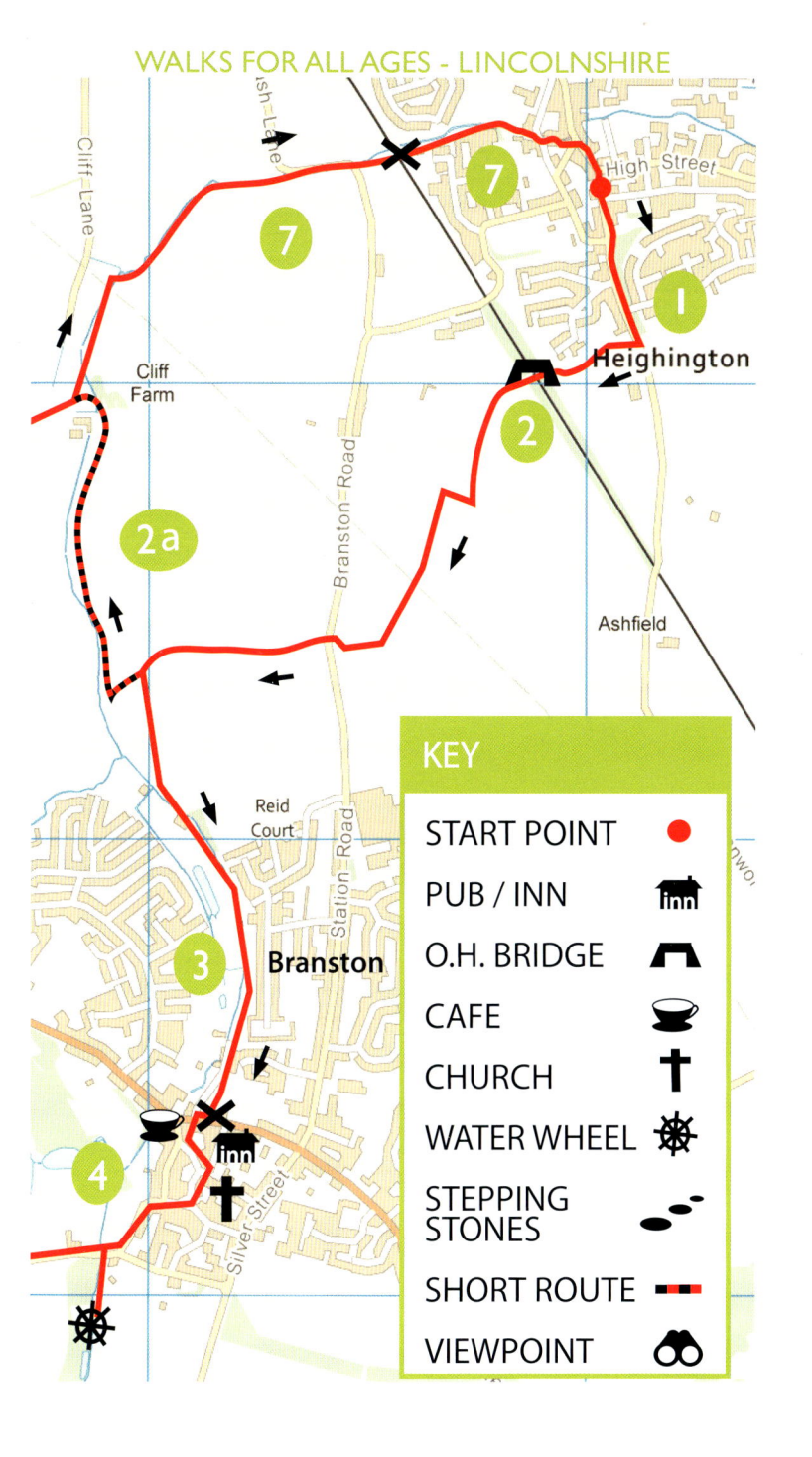

KEY

- START POINT — ●
- PUB / INN
- O.H. BRIDGE
- CAFE
- CHURCH
- WATER WHEEL
- STEPPING STONES
- SHORT ROUTE
- VIEWPOINT

HEIGHINGTON & BRANSTON WALK

1. Once in the car park face the church then turn right, and from the pedestrian exit join the road. Now turn right again uphill. Near the edge of the village take the signed footpath to the right, which briefly joins a road in a housing estate before bearing left to cross a railway.

2. Walk alongside a paddock fence for 100 yards and then turn left over a field. At a grass track (Pudding Busk Lane) go right for a few yards before bearing left again over an arable field aiming for its far right-hand corner where you will come to a road. Follow the path almost opposite heading downhill to reach a path junction.

All Saints Church & Old Rectory

2A. [For the short route back to Heighington keep ahead now over a footbridge and turn right; this will bring you to Cliff Farm. Continue by walking ahead. See 7 (*) below and map.]

3. Otherwise turn left, at first along a field edge path, then a track and finally a lane into Branston village. Cross the main road and bear right a few paces before going left past the inn and café; then go left uphill to the church.

4. Now bear right and right again following the road as it bears left to meet Thacker's Lane. Then go right once more into Hall Lane and the "sculpture" bridge. Next detour left along Waterwheel Lane to see the waterwheel at the end of the garden of the last house; then return to the bridge and turn left.

5. Follow Hall Lane for half a mile and just after some woods turn right onto a signed track. Beyond more trees the path comes to some stepping-stones; cross them and turn left for 300 yards. At a surfaced lane turn right up to the B1189 road.

6. Cross carefully and turn right for 100 yards then take the track on your left heading for Washingborough Top.

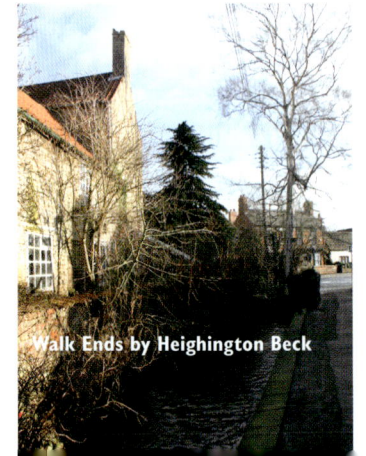

Walk Ends by Heighington Beck

WALKS FOR ALL AGES - LINCOLNSHIRE

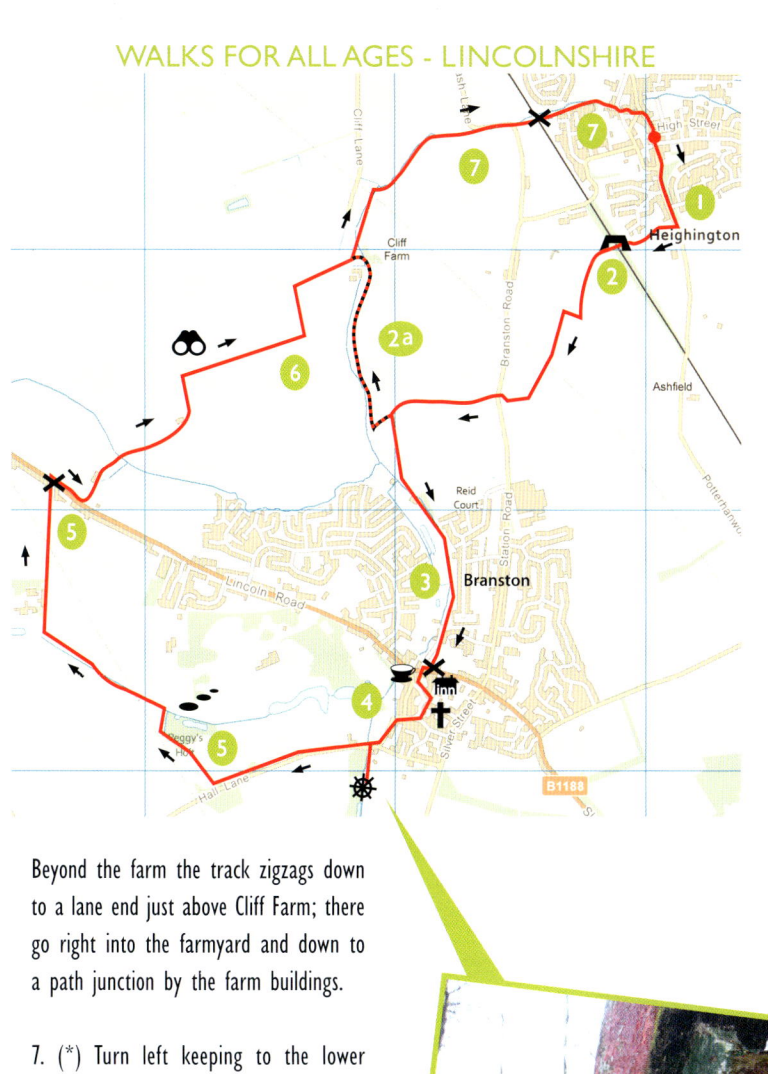

Beyond the farm the track zigzags down to a lane end just above Cliff Farm; there go right into the farmyard and down to a path junction by the farm buildings.

7. (*) Turn left keeping to the lower edge of several meadows to reach a road near Heighington. Follow the cycle way beside the road to the first bend then cross over and continue towards the railway. Cross this carefully before keeping ahead between houses into Heighington, emerging on the road near the mill. Take the surfaced footpath beside a stream almost opposite (just a few paces to your right) and at the next road bear right back to the start.

LINCOLN (UPHILL)

This walk explores the site of the original Roman city, including the environs of the cathedral, with opportunities to visit the city's premier tourist attractions en route.

First a few general comments! Regrettably, for reasons of space, "Uphill" Lincoln's wealth of historic sites are mentioned only briefly; however, there are numerous excellent information boards. This is a fascinating walk however that ricochets back and forth across the centuries from Roman architecture to that of the 21st century and with much for walkers to discover for themselves.

Tennyson Memorial

We begin by setting off down Steep Hill where on our left we see the ancient Norman House (circa 1180) and across the road the Old Harlequin Inn, now a bookshop.

Lincoln Cathedral

At the bottom, on the right, we find the Jew's House and Jew's Court. The former dates from about 1250, and retains many original features, particularly the doorway and upstairs windows. Jew's Court is largely 17th century but upon earlier foundations and was possibly a former synagogue.

Along Dane's Terrace we come to the strikingly modern "Collection" museum (2006) with its stunning modern interior. In contrast again is the Usher Gallery, bequeathed to Lincoln by James Ward Usher, a city sheriff, to house his collection of coins, watches and porcelain. It was officially opened in 1927 by the Prince of Wales using a solid gold key. Inside is the nationally celebrated Peter de Wint painting collection and Alfred, Lord Tennyson memorabilia.

A steep climb up Greenstone Stairs and Greenstone Place brings us through a cathedral close postern gate and past a magnificent mediaeval tithe barn (1440) into Minster Yard. Here, to our right, is the redbrick 14th-century Chancery, home until her death in 1403 of Katherine Swynford, the mistress and eventual wife of John of Gaunt, whilst close to the Priory Gate, another cathedral precinct entrance, is the Tennyson memorial statue. At Eastgate we reach our first visible Roman ruins, their city's eastern gate. Nearby the East Bight follows the line of the city wall, via the site of a Roman aqueduct and on to Newport Arch, the

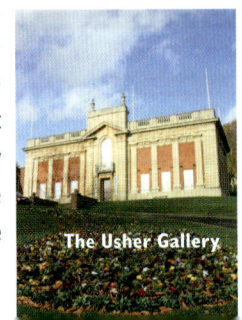

The Usher Gallery

WALKS FOR ALL AGES - LINCOLNSHIRE

Roman city's northern boundary and England's only Roman gateway still in everyday use, though it was almost demolished by a lorry in 1964 (see the picture on the information board.) There is more of Roman Lincoln in West Bight where the Forum boundary, known as the Mint Wall, rises some 25 feet in height.

Then in Westgate we come to St Paul's-in-the-Bail, a church site since about the 4th century, but before that a legionnaires' fortress. In Bailgate itself we enter the Roman Forum, where the positions of its pillars are marked by circular stone setts in the road.

We then return to Castle Square. William the Conqueror built the castle here and evicted 166 Saxon families to do so. Completed in 1068, it has of course been altered and added to over the centuries – especially the 12th and 13th – but has always been a prison with the Georgian gaol dating from 1787 and a unique Victorian prison chapel added in 1845. The castle also houses one of only four surviving copies of the Magna Carta of 1215.

Nothing quite prepares the visitor passing through the 14th-century Exchequer Gate for the close-up view of the stupendous, man-made stone cliff that is the cathedral's west front. The houses to the left were the first in the city to have street numbers and are appropriately called the "Number Houses".

THE BASICS

Distance in miles & km: 1¾ miles: 3 kilometres.
Gradient: One steep descent and one steep climb.
Severity: Easy except for Steep Hill and Greenstone Stairs.
Approx time to walk: 75 mins.
Stiles: None.
Maps: OS Explorer 272 or (better) a street map from the tourist office.
Path description: Entirely urban.
Start Point: Castle Square, Lincoln. LN1 3AA (GR 976717)
Parking: Castle Square but there are larger car parks in Westgate.
Dog friendly: Entire route is in an urban environment.
Public toilets: Castle Hill.
Nearest food: Plentiful cafés, inns, tearooms and restaurants.

LINCOLN (UPHILL) WALK

The cathedral's basic history and vicissitudes, through fire in 1141 and earthquake in 1185, followed by Bishop Hugh's rebuilding, are well known but it is one of England's grandest religious buildings, so any visit will be richly rewarding. Particularly noteworthy are the imposing chapter house and the Dean's Eye window in the north transept. And in the Angel Choir look out for the famous "Lincoln Imp", the unofficial symbol of both the cathedral and the city. On the outside another unusual visitor attraction recently has been the peregrines nesting on the south transept.

The Number Houses

The Collection, Usher Gallery, cathedral and castle are all recommended visits during or after the walk. Street maps are available from the TIC on Castle Square or a map-dispensing machine outside the adjacent church.

NOTE. The Steep Hill and Greenstone Stairs sections (1 to 3) may be omitted, along with much of interest too, by walking through the Exchequer Gate and along Minster Yard to pick up the main route at section 3 (see map). Otherwise:

1. From outside the tourist office head down Steep Hill immediately opposite. Continue until the road widens and at Jew's Court you can turn left along Danes Terrace.

2. Walk past the Collection museum and across the road into the Temple Gardens surrounding the Usher Gallery. Bear right down to the main gate and there

The Jew's House

go left up Lindum Road for 200 yards. Now bear left again for the ascent of the 55 steps of the Greenstone Stairs and after an old postern gate continue up the steep(ish) Greenstone Place to emerge opposite the cathedral.

3. Keep forward along the cathedral's eastern end to the Tennyson statue near the Priory Gate and cross the road to the Roman East Gate site outside the Lincoln Hotel. Turn left and in a few yards go right along East Bight to reach the Newport Arch at the end of Bailgate.

4. Cross into Chapel Lane opposite and in 100 yards go left along West Bight into Westgate.

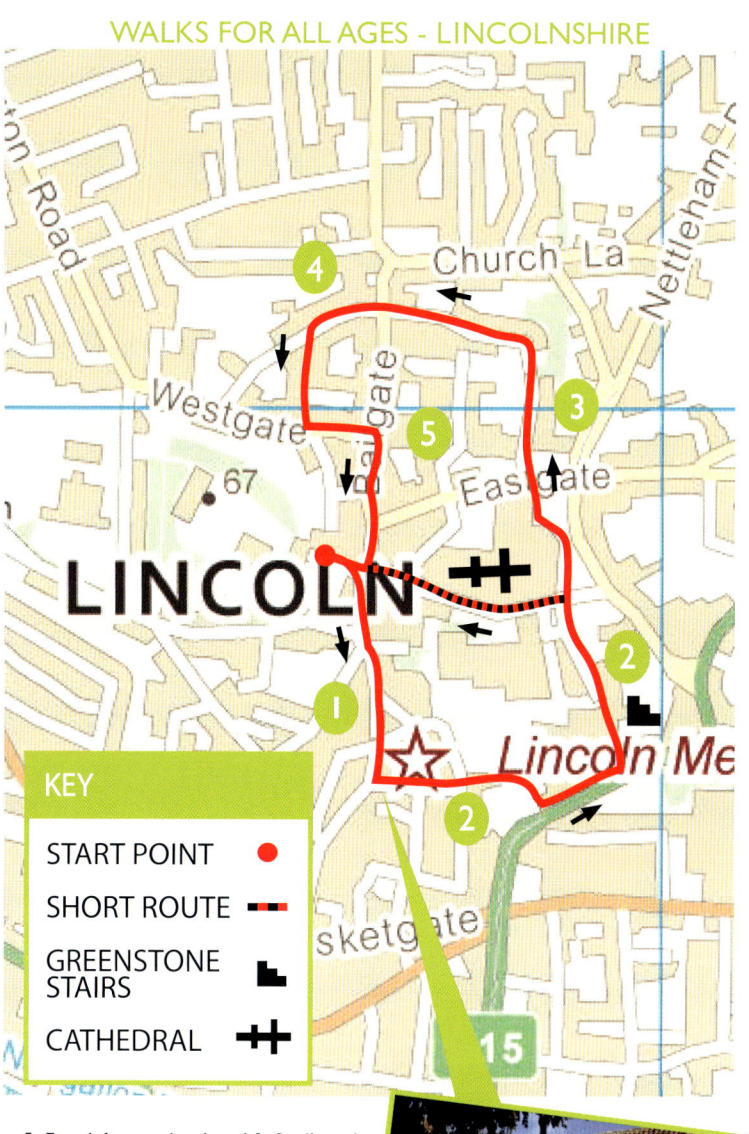

WALKS FOR ALL AGES - LINCOLNSHIRE

KEY

- START POINT ●
- SHORT ROUTE ▬▬
- GREENSTONE STAIRS ▟
- CATHEDRAL ✚

5. Turn left past the site of St Paul's and at Bailgate bear right to return to the start at Castle Hill.

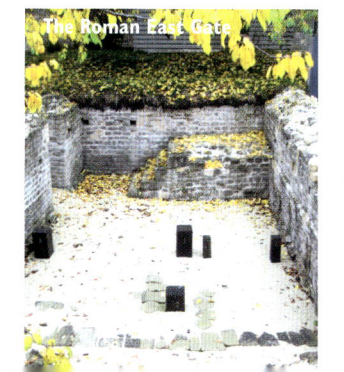

The Roman East Gate

SOUTH & NORTH RAUCEBY

This is quite a cultural ramble for it visits some unusual outdoor sculptures sponsored by North Kesteven District Council (NKDC).

North and South Rauceby lie just west of Sleaford and in their administrative area NKDC have commissioned original sculptures from local artists for outdoor display. Many are located along specially developed "Stepping Out" country walks also developed by NKDC. Our ramble takes advantage of both these initiatives.

A foretaste of these projects is seen as we arrive via either of the Rauceby's to start the walk, for whichever way we come we pass a village name sign featuring the "Lost Sheep" — a reference to the significance of sheep-rearing locally.

The first sculpture visited on the walk itself is "In the Field" in Southgate Spinney, overlooking South Rauceby's old quarry. This also portrays local farming and wildlife subjects, and includes a bustard (about which more below) superimposed onto a map-like arrangement of fields.

"In The Field"

Just after Hall Farm we find the "Boggart Bench"; a sculpture produced with the help of local volunteers. As the "Boggart" is an impish figure of local folklore who lives underground he hides around the back of the main carving with its recumbent shepherd and Rauceby village on a hilltop. There are extensive views here over the valley of the River Slea — and of distant Sleaford itself.

Outside Rauceby Hall is the bearded "Sleeping Shepherd", with something of the legendary "Green Man" fertility symbol about him. He again rests with sheep and lambs close by, but somewhat humorously the artist has carved lots of mint round the back!

The Boggart Bench

The Boggart

WALKS FOR ALL AGES - LINCOLNSHIRE

Our final sculpture — the "Fieldstone" — is placed on the roadside verge near North Rauceby church. Again there is an agricultural subject with ears of wheat and field birds including a pheasant.

St Peter's Church at North Rauceby has one of the best examples of a Lincolnshire architectural speciality, the broach spire. Not only that but it is also one of the earliest and dates from the 13th century. Broach spires are unusual in that they rise directly from the edges of the tower walls without a parapet. On the nearby green the ancient village cross, restored in 1861, has a small tabernacle on the top.

Back in South Rauceby the walk passes close to the old windmill that was built in 1841 and working until the 1930s.

And finally — the Bustard Inn! The story goes that this 1860 inn got its name in commemoration of the last bustard in Lincolnshire, which was shot nearby.

THE BASICS

Distance in miles & km: 3¼ or 4¼ miles: 5 or 7 kilometres.
Gradient: Short uphill sections but mostly level.
Severity: Easy.
Approx time to walk: 90 mins or 120 mins.
Stiles: 2.
Maps: OS Landranger 130 (Grantham): Explorer 272.
Path description: Country lanes, farm tracks and meadows.
Start Point: The Bustard Inn, South Rauceby. LN1 3AA (GR 026456)
Parking: At start; by permission of the landlord.
Dog friendly: OK except where there is stock in fields.
Public toilets: None. Only at inn.
Nearest food: Bustard Inn.

SOUTH & NORTH RAUCEBY MAP

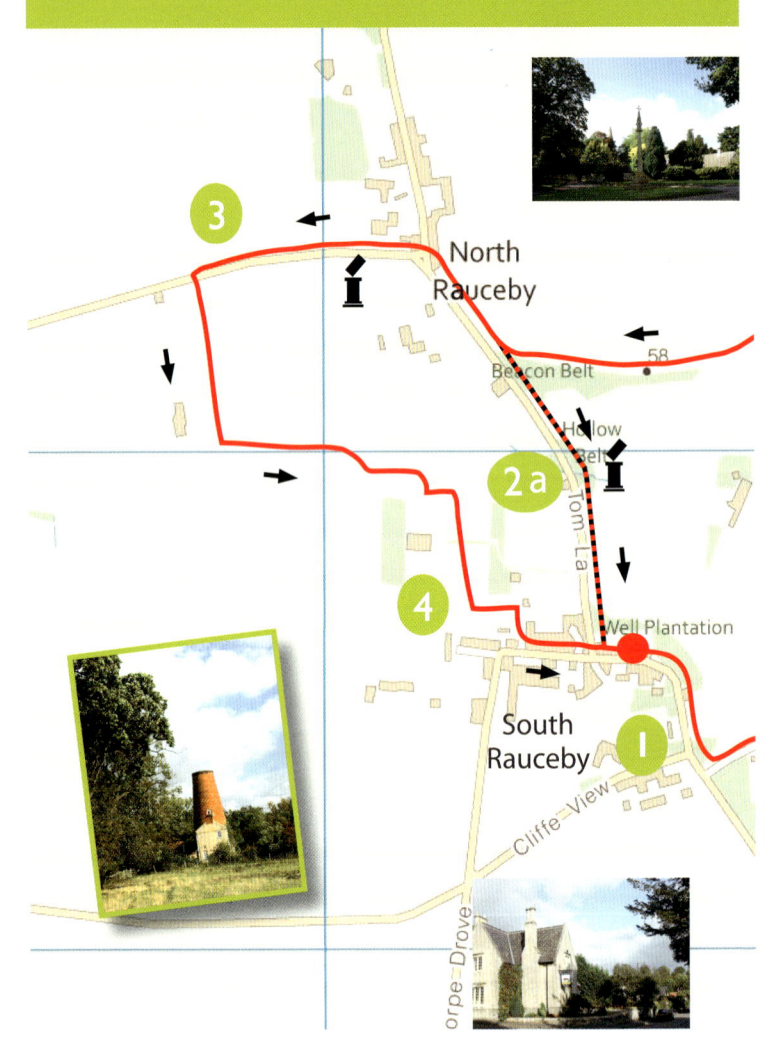

NOTES. Not all North Kesteven District Council's "Stepping Out" footpaths are shown on OS maps. Some may be muddy!

1. Exit the inn car park and turn left, then left once more across the front of the inn. Walk downhill and when you reach Pinfold Lane turn left again. At the end keep ahead onto the access road for Hall Farm where, almost at once, a footpath on the right heads into the trees of Southgate Spinney. Our first sculpture — "In the Field" — is 100 yards into these woods. Visit and return!

2. Carry on towards Hall Farm and follow the track as it bears right just before the farmyard. The track soon bends left, then goes through some trees before bearing right again. At a track junction is the "Boggart" sculpture. From here keep forward to a second

WALKS FOR ALL AGES - LINCOLNSHIRE

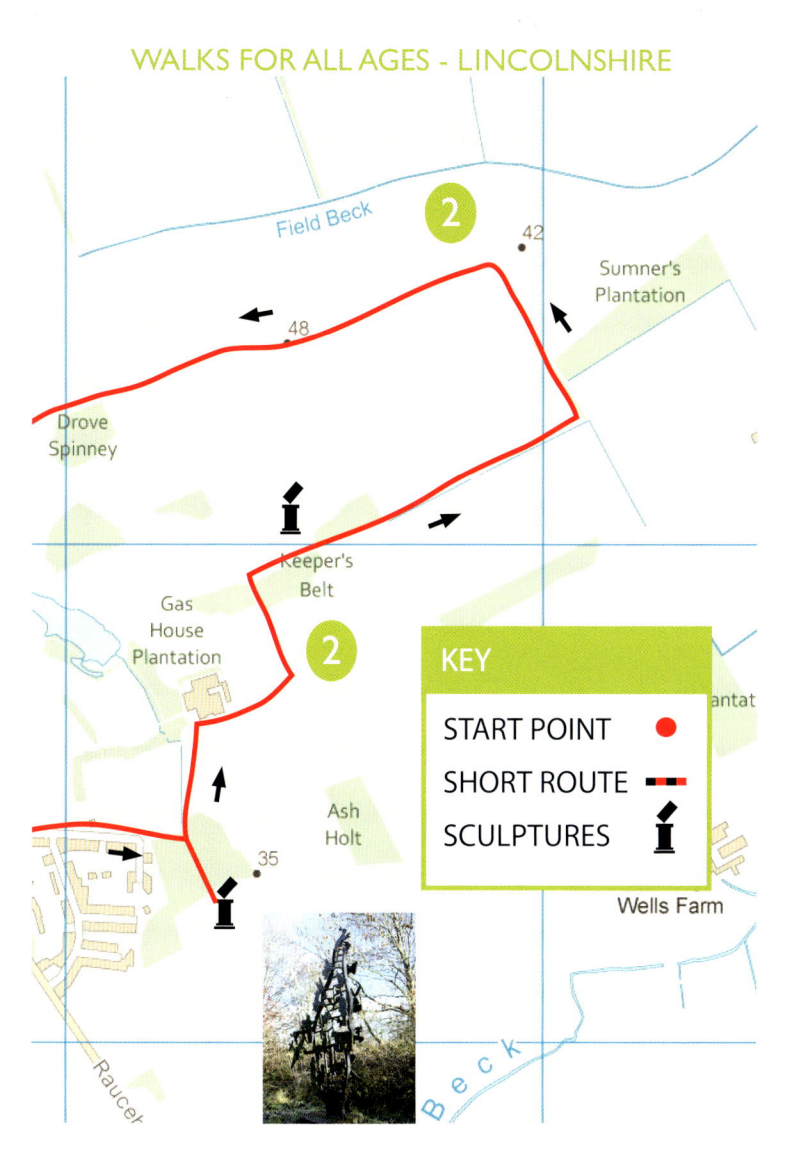

junction, by some electricity wires, and turn left on an uphill grass track. When another wide, grassy lane is met (Drove Lane) turn left again for approximately a mile until you reach the road near North Rauceby.

2A. Built into the wall corner here is an unusual stone seat — most welcome if you need a "breather"! A few yards away to the left now is Rauceby Hall entrance and our third sculpture — the "Sleeping Shepherd". (The short route then continues along the road back to the inn.)

3. For the longer route return to the end of Drove Lane and keep ahead to the village green with its cross at North Rauceby, there turning left along Church Lane to pass the "Fieldstone" carving. Continue for a further quarter of a mile

SOUTH & NORTH RAUCEBY WALK

and then turn left into the entrance for Glebe Farm. Follow the access lane to a metal gate just beyond the farmhouse.

4. Go through and turn left along a grass track to a second gate and a stile. In the large meadow beyond gradually veer right and keep right once past the grounds of a large house. (There's a waymark on the corner of the garden wall.) Cross the house drive, heading downhill until Rauceby mill appears to your left. Now bear left down to a gate just beyond some wooden huts. At the road beyond turn left back to The Bustard.

North Rauceby

WALKS FOR ALL AGES - LINCOLNSHIRE

TATTERSHALL & CONINGSBY

This short route explores the two historic villages of Tattershall and Coningsby. The local attractions of Tattershall Castle (National Trust) and the Battle of Britain Memorial Flight museum make it an ideal element of a family day out.

We begin from Tattershall's busy Market Place with its mediaeval cross and striking millennium sundial. Nearby (opposite the Fortescue Arms) are the remains of the Tattershall College of priests, which probably also served as a schoolroom, and was founded by Ralph Cromwell, builder of the nearby castle and church.

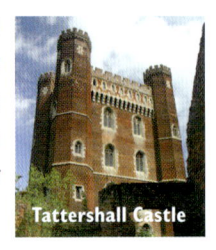

Tattershall Castle

Tattershall Castle is not only one of Lincolnshire's best-known landmarks but also one of England's most important Tudor brick buildings. It was begun in 1434 by Ralph Lord Cromwell, who acquired his riches whilst Treasurer of England to Henry VI. The tower – which has fabulous views from the roof – stands 110 feet high, a colossal undertaking for 15th-century builders, and contemporary accounts record that 320,000 bricks were needed for the dungeons alone! Internally derelict by the early 20th century, it was purchased and restored by Lord Curzon of Kedleston in 1911 and bequeathed to the National Trust upon his death in 1925. (There is an admission charge to non-members of the NT.)

Market Place

Ralph Cromwell also founded the adjacent Holy Trinity church in 1439. This beautiful building took thirty years to erect so was incomplete when Cromwell died in 1455. It is one of Lincolnshire's largest parish churches and its splendour (intended of course!) again emphasises its patron's wealth. Unusually, all the windows are of clear glass and so the interior is very light. It is believed that the original mediaeval glass was sold in 1754 because the vicar of the time had poor eyesight and needed better lighting to help him read the lessons. Opposite the church are attractive Bede Houses dating from the early 16th century. They are successors to those established by Cromwell in AD1440 – but there had been earlier ones on the site even then.

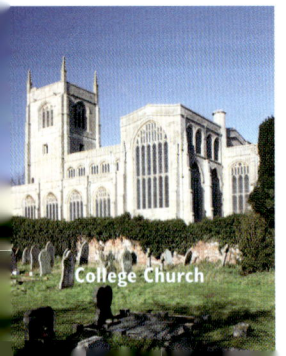

College Church

WALKS FOR ALL AGES - LINCOLNSHIRE

Just off route as we reach Coningsby — and worth visiting after the walk — is the Battle of Britain Memorial Flight. This was established in 1957 with a museum and hangars for its Lancaster bomber and Spitfire and Hurricane fighter aircraft. On summer weekends it is often possible to see these in close-up action as they set off to, or return from, air displays.

Another unique feature of Coningsby is St Michael's Church and its famous one-handed clock, measuring sixteen feet across and believed to be the biggest in the world.

To the south of Horncastle much of the River Bain, which flows through both Tattershall and Coningsby, was canalised (i.e. straightened) to become the Horncastle Canal. This was begun in 1796 and completed in 1802. On reaching Tattershall the canal branched away from the Bain to join the Witham just north of Tattershall Bridge; passenger boats could then sail up or down river to Lincoln or Boston. It closed in 1878 and there is an abandoned section beside Tattershall castle car park. The second half of the walk is beside this canal, though nowadays it doesn't really look like one. Nevertheless, the footpath offers lovely views of Coningsby church and its clock and finally of Tattershall Castle again.

THE BASICS

Distance in miles & km: 2¼ miles: 3.5 kilometres.
Gradient: level throughout.
Severity: Easy.
Approx time to walk: 75 mins.
Stiles: None.
Maps: OS Landranger 122 (Skegness): Explorer 261.
Path description: Village pavements and grass paths.
Start Point: Tattershall Market Place. LN4 4NJ (GR 213578)
Parking: Tattershall Market Place.
Dog friendly: In parts; on leads at roads etc.
Public toilets: Coningsby village car park. Or at the castle, local inns.
Nearest food: Inns & cafés in both villages. Tea sometimes available in Tattershall church.

TATTERSHALL & CONINGSBY WALK

NOTE. In addition to Tattershall Market Place there is more parking en route near the castle and church (GR213577).

1. Cross the road opposite the Fortescue Arms to the entrance of Tattershall College, then turn right and in a few yards take the footpath on the left. This crosses the abandoned Horncastle canal into the NT castle car park, which gives access to both church and castle. Turn left to a footbridge over the weir at the River Bain.
(Readers parking here should join the walk at this footbridge.)

Market Place

2. After crossing the river turn right for 100 yards to a waymark for a footpath going off to the left. Follow this past some lakes and keep ahead to reach a road opposite Coningsby cemetery. (The Battle of Britain Memorial Flight is a few yards to your right.) Turn left through the village to the road junction by the church.

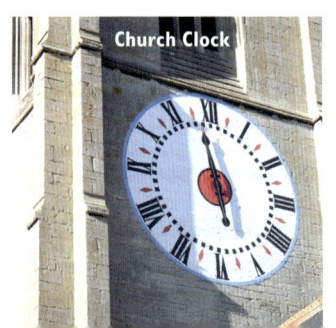

3. Turn right here to cross the road at the pedestrian crossing and then continue to a footpath (Masons Lane) on the left near the Black Swan. Follow this to the river/canal and cross the footbridge. Go through the kissing gate on the left and walk beside the canal to reach another road.

4. Cross this and turn left over the bridge; then at once go right with the river/canal on your right. From the weir and bridge at the castle car park retrace the outward route to your car.

St Michael's Church

Church Clock

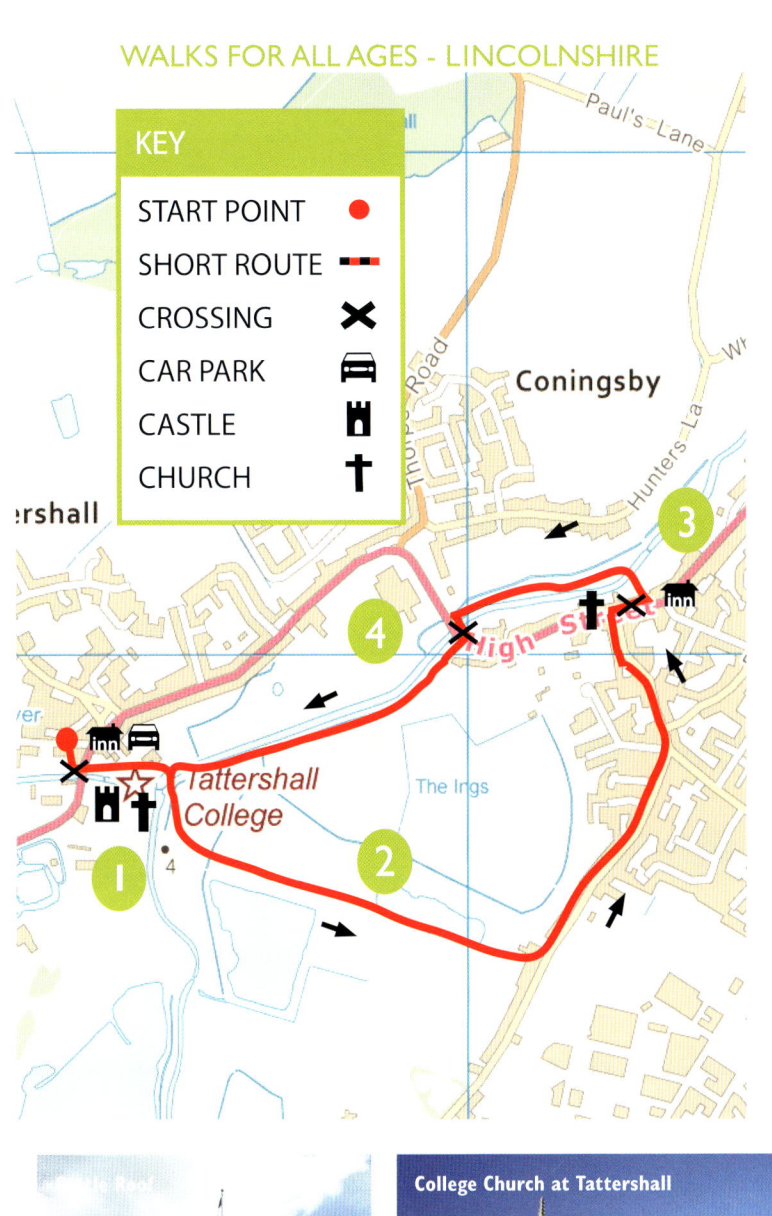

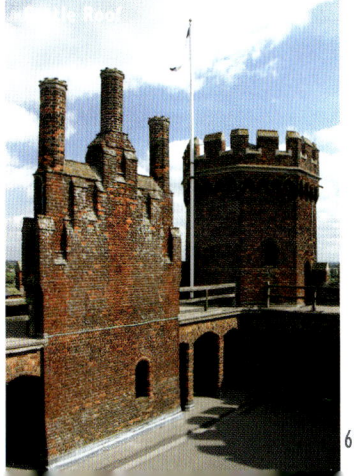

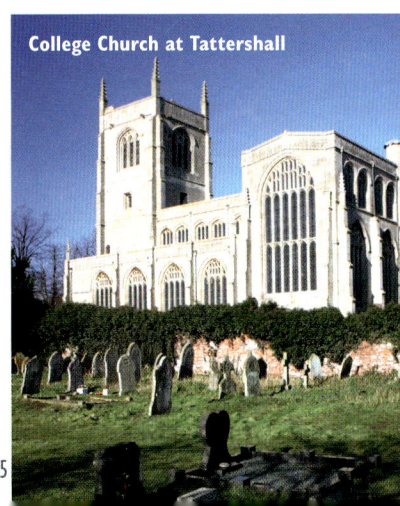

WALKS FOR ALL AGES - LINCOLNSHIRE

KEY

- START POINT — ●
- SHORT ROUTE — ▬▬
- CROSSING — ✗
- CAR PARK
- CASTLE
- CHURCH — ✝

College Church at Tattershall

TEALBY

With its reputation as the prettiest village in the Wolds. Tealby is well worth visiting. But first we explore some easy local footpaths.

Lying within the Wolds Area of Outstanding Natural Beauty and astride the Viking Way long-distance trail, Tealby attracts ramblers all year round to its many fine walks. Our short outing begins from the thatched, mud-and-stud King's Head Inn dating from around 1367. It's the oldest thatched inn in Lincolnshire and, apart from the church, Tealby's oldest building.

King's Head Inn

However, the 21st century's undisturbed atmosphere belies a quite industrial history. Recorded as Tavelesbi in the Domesday Book of 1086, the village apparently had twelve watermills. These were powered by the infant River Rase, which springs from the steep slopes of Bully Hill some two miles to the east and quickly becomes quite a substantial stream. The approach from the High Street and Bully Hill is along Papermill Lane, a name that recalls Tealby's one-time importance for paper production.

All Saints churchyard on the hilltop has fine views over the cottages below towards the expanses of Bayons Park beyond. Built from local, browny-gold ironstone, the church has a Norman tower, Early English and Decorated work and Tennyson family memorials inside. It was restored in 1871.

All Saints Church

The Tennysons were the leading family here from the 1780s, their most well-known member (in Tealby at any rate) being Charles Tennyson d'Eyncourt, uncle to Alfred the poet from Somersby. Charles inherited the Bayons estate in 1835 since it was anticipated that he, rather than his brother George (Alfred's father), would potentially bring greater distinction to the family name. (Quite wrongly as things turned out!) In the park Charles built his pseudo-Gothic Bayons Manor, a moated replica of a mediaeval castle, between 1836 and 1842 but it was badly damaged during service as a World War II troops billet, fell into disrepair and was demolished in 1965.

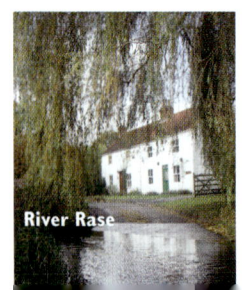

River Rase 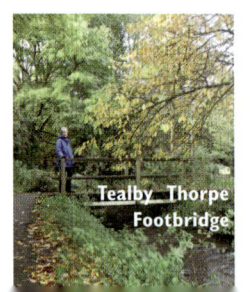 | *Tealby Thorpe Footbridge* 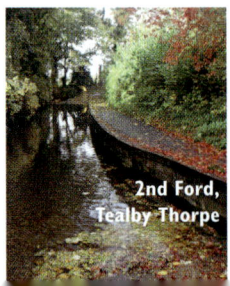 | *2nd Ford, Tealby Thorpe*

WALKS FOR ALL AGES - LINCOLNSHIRE

Charles also helped Tealby by paying for a new school in 1856 and was probably its architect too, as he was then an MP and the hammer-beam roof inside is very similar to that in Westminster Hall. He also paid for much of the church restoration in the 1870s and sixty years later the family also provided the village Memorial Hall on Beck Hill.

A mile to the west, down a narrow "No Through Road" lies the hidden hamlet of Tealby Thorpe. A mill still stands here but the appeal comes from its remoteness and two picturesque fords at the River Rase.

As we return into Tealby we pass by the roadside another surviving watermill at Watermill House. (Do note however that it is a private residence!) Nearer to the inn is the late-18th-century Linden House with its gothic, pointed-window extension: this was the village doctor's surgery until 1949.

NOTE. Readers may park at the King's Head by kind permission of the landlord.

Tealby Church

THE BASICS

Distance in miles & km: 2½ miles: 4 kilometres.
Gradient: Level but gentle climbs within Tealby village.
Severity: Easy.
Approx time to walk: 75 mins.
Stiles: None.
Maps: OS Landranger 113 (Grimsby): Explorer 282.
Path description: Country lanes, meadows, village pavements, roads.
Start Point: King's Head, Tealby. LN8 3YA (GR 156904)
Parking: King's Head, Tealby.
Dog friendly: Off leads only on meadow sections.
Public toilets: None – try inn.
Nearest food: The King's Head, Tealby.

TEALBY WALK

1. Leave the inn car park and turn right and at the lane end cross a footbridge over the River Rase onto a fenced path in Bayons Park. On reaching a stony track turn right and walk to the public road. Continue ahead along the pavement opposite for approximately a quarter of a mile to a "T" junction and then turn right along the "No Through Road" into Tealby Thorpe.

The Kings Head

2. At the first ford bear left on a waterside path to a footbridge, go across and turn left – soon along another raised waterside path. 200 yards after rejoining the surfaced road look for a footpath sign and kissing gate on the right; just near a "Try Your Brakes" sign.

3. Turn right keeping to the right-hand side of a long meadow to a second kissing gate and footpath sign then follow a fenced path to a three-way footpath sign. Still keep ahead through trees and after another kissing gate bear right along the edge of another meadow. Soon two more kissing gates, very close together, lead onto a road (Sandy Lane). Turn left again to pass Watermill House and arrive back at the King's Head.

4. Before returning to the inn, first explore Tealby village by bearing left uphill to take the narrow lane on the left of the butchers shop (Church Lane). At the top carefully cross Rasen Road (B1203) and turn right, soon branching left into the lane behind the church. Almost immediately bear right up steps (12) into the churchyard and walk round the tower for a wonderful view across the village and Bayons Park. Leave by more steps (19) and re-cross the B1203 into Beck Hill.

Tealby Thorpe

All Saint's Tower

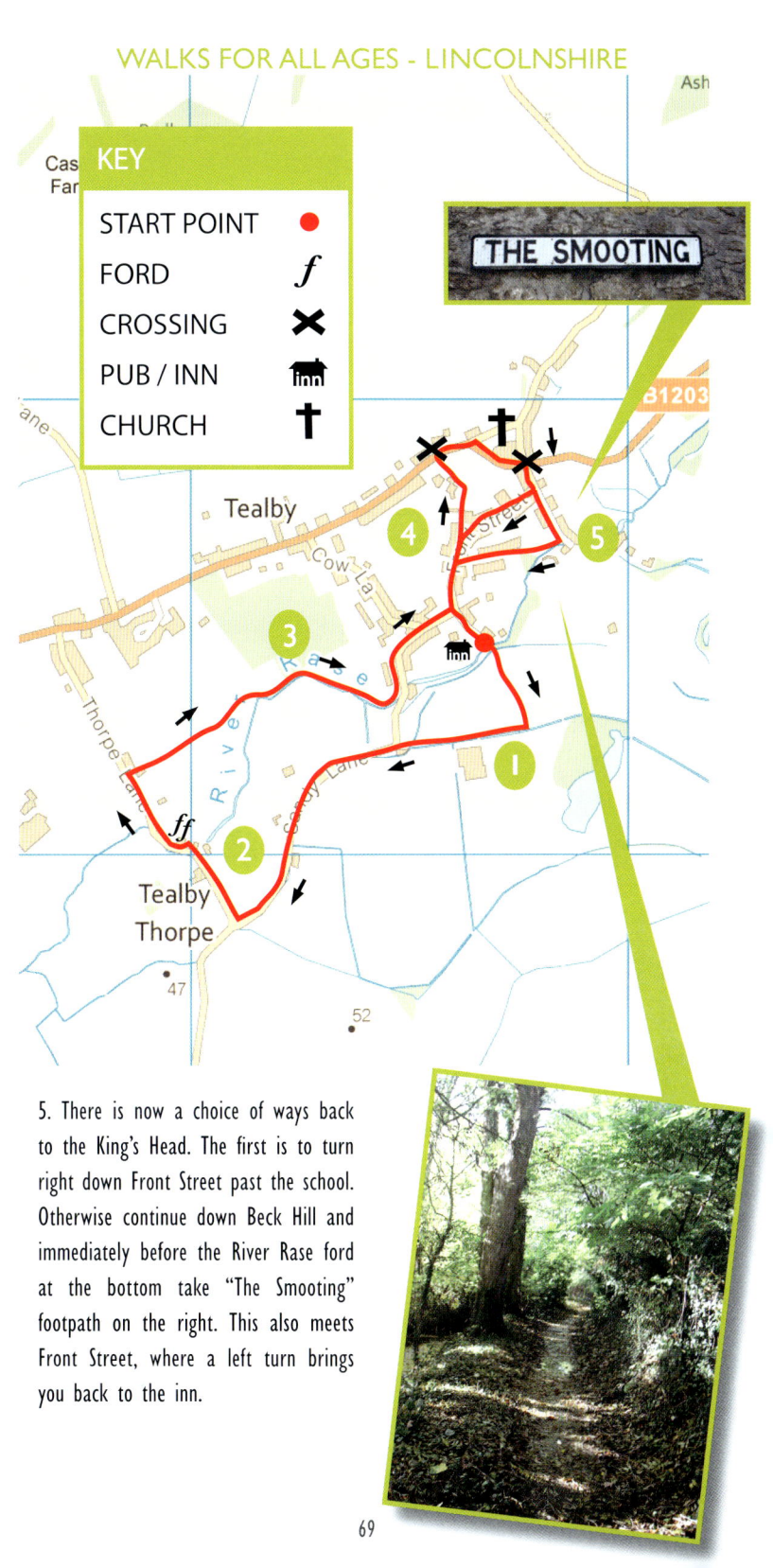

WALKS FOR ALL AGES - LINCOLNSHIRE

KEY

START POINT	●
FORD	f
CROSSING	✕
PUB / INN	inn
CHURCH	†

5. There is now a choice of ways back to the King's Head. The first is to turn right down Front Street past the school. Otherwise continue down Beck Hill and immediately before the River Rase ford at the bottom take "The Smooting" footpath on the right. This also meets Front Street, where a left turn brings you back to the inn.

TETNEY LOCK

Situated on Lincolnshire's north-east coast, this bracing walk is partially beside the Louth Navigation. There are impressive views over the mighty Humber Estuary to Spurn Point.

The Louth Navigation was built between 1765 and 1770 at a cost of £28,000 and linked the town with Tetney Lock. There it met the tidal Tetney Haven, so giving it direct access to the Humber, and thence onwards to inland ports. The Navigation – the term for the "straightened" river (in this case the Lud) as opposed to a completely newly dug canal – was deliberately constructed considerably wider than was usual for canals. This allowed vessels such as Humber keels to sail directly into Louth without incurring costly delays by having to transfer cargoes onto smaller barges. This proved so successful that Louth became, for a while, a busier port than Grimsby.

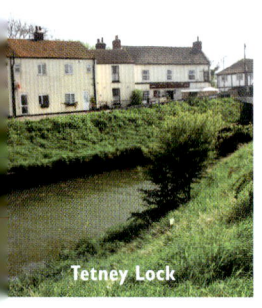

Aerial View of Tetney Lock

The walk commences at Tetney Lock where the navigation's sea lock blocked the inflow of salt water from the Haven. The flatness of the surrounding countryside meant that no further lock was needed for the next seven miles upstream, but six were required during the final three miles to Louth's Riverhead. Even after the Great Northern Railway built their Grimsby to Peterborough line through Louth in 1848 the navigation remained in business, but the disastrous Louth Flood of 29th May 1920 changed all that. There was immense damage at Louth Riverhead and the navigation company simply could not afford the cost of repairs, so trade ceased virtually overnight although formal closure was not until June 1924. At Tetney Lock the lane by the north bank is still called "The Wharf" and an information board is nearby.

Tetney Lock

A short distance away, close to the Tetney Drain, are some early 19th-century Coastguard Cottages. Their location, now a mile from the sea, clearly demonstrates the growth of the coastal marshes over the last two hundred years. Close by is an attractive Primitive Methodist Chapel dated 1864. The Crown and Anchor inn is mid-19th century too.

Tetney Drain

WALKS FOR ALL AGES - LINCOLNSHIRE

Once we climb onto the Humber bank the views open up spectacularly and offer an opportunity to spot some of the wildlife of the estuary marshes. Since 1975 some 1,500 hectares of marsh and dunes around Tetney Haven has been an RSPB reserve and there is an information board at the sluice where we cross the Haven before returning to Tetney Lock.

There's always something of interest out on the Humber too, with shipping heading to and from the inland ports of Grimsby, Immingham, Hull and Goole. The estuary's size reflects the fact that it drains substantial parts of central and northern England, and with tributaries from as far away as the Staffordshire moors and Yorkshire Dales it collects one-fifth of England's fresh water.

Clearly visible too are the Haile Sand (nearer) and Bull Sand (distant) Forts guarding the main river channels. These were built during World War I from reinforced concrete and steel armour plating to ward off a new threat to shipping – that of submarines. Also visible is Spurn Point, some 5½ miles away as the crow flies.

THE BASICS

Distance in miles & km: 4½ miles: 7 kilometres.
Gradient: Level.
Severity: Easy.
Approx time to walk: 120 mins.
Stiles: 4.
Maps: OS Landranger 113 (Grimsby): Explorer 283.
Path description: Lanes, farm tracks, sea & canal embankments.
Start Point: Tetney Lock bridge. DN36 5UW (GR 343022)
Parking: At inn with landlord's/manager's permission; or roadside nearby.
Dog friendly: Best on leads.
Public toilets: None.
Nearest food: The Crown and Anchor, Tetney Lock.

TETNEY LOCK WALK

This walk is best done on a clear day; also bring binoculars for bird and ship watching!

1. Cross the bridge in front of the inn and follow the road to the next bridge over the Tetney Drain. Cross this too and turn right along the lane running parallel with the water channel. (You can use the drain's lower flood bank or the lane.) Continue until just after a pumping station where the lane bends left.

2. Turn along it to pass a farm where the lane becomes a track. Keep forward to the former site of Low Farm and a concrete step-stile at the gate ahead. Climb over and in a few yards at a track junction turn right. Leave the track almost at once onto the grass footpath ahead that leads to a footbridge and the sea bank. From the top the panorama of the Humber Estuary, its forts, Tetney Haven and Spurn Point are all suddenly revealed.

3. Turn right and after 1¼ miles you will reach the Tetney Haven again. A few paces to your left is the RSPB information board and a bridge across the Haven. Once across, walk forward to a stile by a gate and then on to a WWII pillbox.

Tetney Haven

4. Bear right now to a second stile by another gate. All that is needed now is to simply follow the Haven back inland on either the upper or lower embankment. In a mile or so a final stile gives onto a short lane leading back to the start.

RSPB Info Board

On The Humber Bank

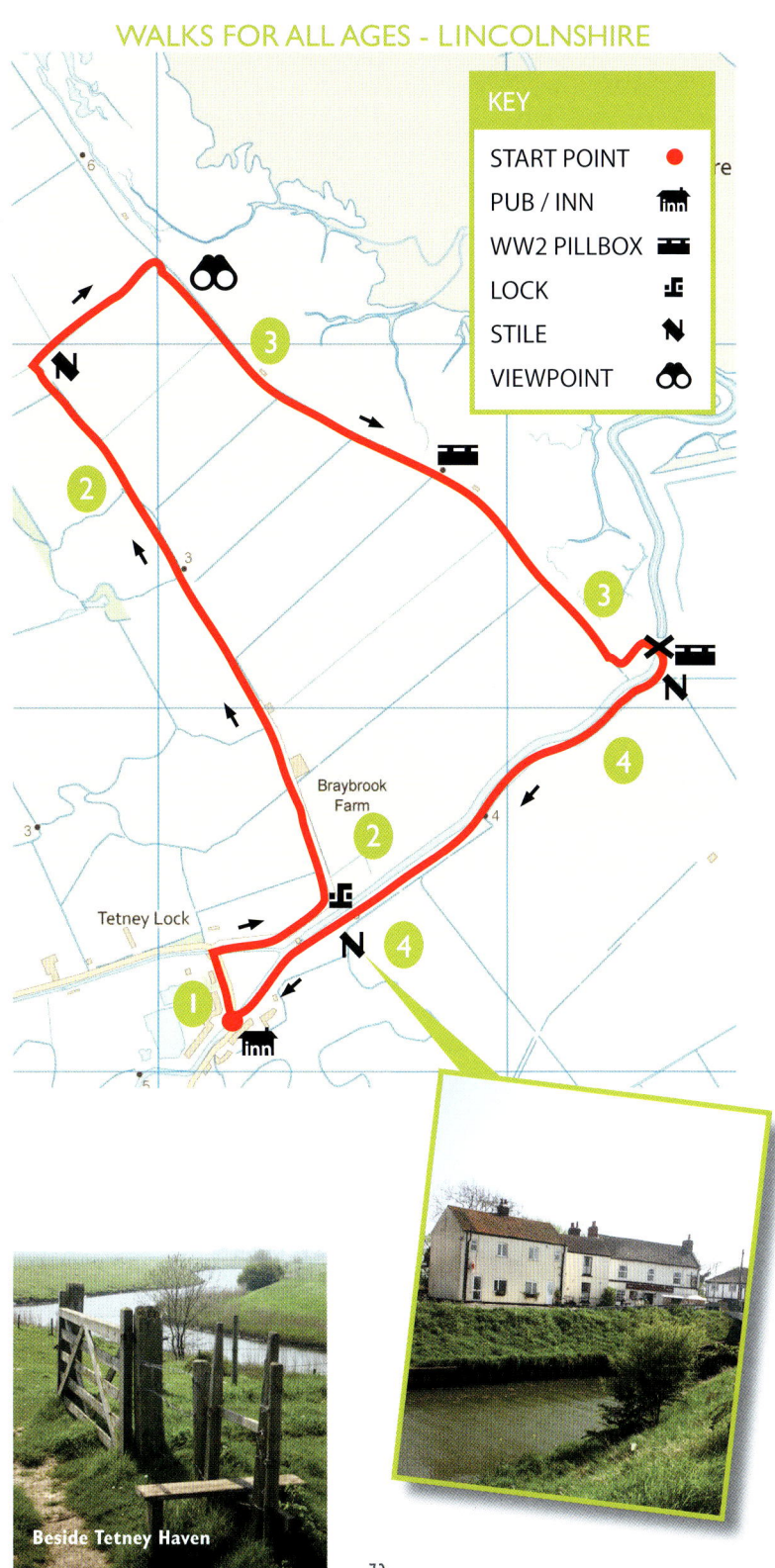

WALKS FOR ALL AGES - LINCOLNSHIRE

KEY
- START POINT
- PUB / INN
- WW2 PILLBOX
- LOCK
- STILE
- VIEWPOINT

Braybrook Farm

Tetney Lock

Beside Tetney Haven

73

MARKET DEEPING

This simple walk alongside the River Welland also offers even shorter options since at Deeping Gate bridges across the River Welland link with the return section of this "there-and-back" route beside the river.

Although essentially a village walk, this route is nevertheless one of contrasts and from this most southern part of Lincolnshire we (briefly!) stray into Cambridgeshire. Information boards for the local "Welland Walk" are seen en route.

Deeping Gate Bridge

The Market Deeping district has been settled since at least the Bronze Age. And the Romans were here too! This is hardly surprising since their Car Dyke, which linked the River Nene near Peterborough to the Witham at Lincoln, intersected with the Welland close to Deeping Gate Bridge. Also their King Street road ran only a couple of miles to the west.

The local architecture reflects the location of these villages on the fringes of the limestone belt, and many lovely buildings, both grand and modest, are (just like beautiful Stamford nearby) built of this local stone.

High Street Market Deeping

Both Market Deeping and Deeping St James are well known for their links with the Wake family, the lords of Bourne and Deeping. One of their number was Joan, the Fair Maid of Kent who married the Black Prince, but the most famous family member was Hereward the Wake, who in the late 12th century led a rebellion against the invading Normans under William the Conqueror.

There is important industrial archaeology here too, for the River Welland was "canalised" in the 17th century to become possibly England's first canal. The Welland rises near Market Harborough but is a substantial river on entering Lincolnshire at Stamford, which was a thriving trading centre by the reign of Elizabeth I. Even then the Welland had been part of a time-honoured trade route to northern Europe, but using the river was becoming increasingly difficult. In 1571 an Act of Parliament authorised improvements to make it navigable between Stamford and the sea, but work only began in the early 17th century and was not complete until the

The River Welland

WALKS FOR ALL AGES - LINCOLNSHIRE

1660s. Traces of one of the early locks from that time are seen near the first footbridge passed on the walk. The lock at Scout Island occupies the site of the first of twelve between Deeping and Stamford. Also at Deeping Gate is the beautiful, arched river bridge built in 1651.

There was a much earlier church at Deeping St James than the one we see today. Its large size, however, far bigger than one would normally expect in a village, is because it was first the church of a Benedictine priory founded here in 1139. In the chancel there still remain the seats (sedilia) for the monks, who probably never numbered more than a dozen. The priory itself was closed at the Dissolution of 1539 but as today's parish church it still incorporates some early 14th-century windows plus an 18th-century tower and spire.

Just outside the churchyard, however, is a real curiosity – the former village market cross. In 1819 this became the village lock-up and an information board describes how a hole in its ancient oak door was used to give prisoners a drink.

Further on at Scout Island the local Rotary club has recently improved access to the island, cleared undergrowth, made new paths and provided benches and bird and bat boxes.

THE BASICS

Distance in miles & km: 4¼ miles: 6.5 kilometres.
Gradient: Level throughout.
Severity: Easy.
Approx time to walk: 120 mins.
Stiles: None.
Maps: OS Landranger 142: Explorer 235.
Path description:
Start Point: Market Place, Market Deeping. PE6 8EA (GR 139099)
Parking: Market Place, Market Deeping.
Dog friendly: Best on leads throughout.
Public toilets: The Precinct, Market Deeping.
Nearest food: The Bell Inn, The Boundary Fish & Chip Shop.

MARKET DEEPING WALK

KEY
- START POINT ●
- PUB / INN
- LOCK-UP
- CROSSING ✗

1. Leave the Market Place and head eastwards along High Street to a roundabout. Continue towards Deeping St James and on reaching a road junction keep ahead again. You will soon now come alongside the river at a weir and footbridge and by an old lock. Carry on to Deeping Gate and the old road bridge.

2. Just beyond that and another footbridge, take a left turn into Hereward Way. After 20 yards turn right along an enclosed footpath past the cemetery and enter Deeping St James churchyard.

3. Leave the churchyard by its far right-hand corner and beyond the lock-up bear left along Eastgate. At the junction with Stowgate Road (the B1166 goes left here) turn right along an enclosed footpath to a footbridge onto Scout Island. Follow a path to a second footbridge and cross the river onto it's far bank.
(You are now in Cambridgeshire!)

4. Bear right on the riverside path for about ¾ of a mile to a kissing gate and a road.

WALKS FOR ALL AGES - LINCOLNSHIRE

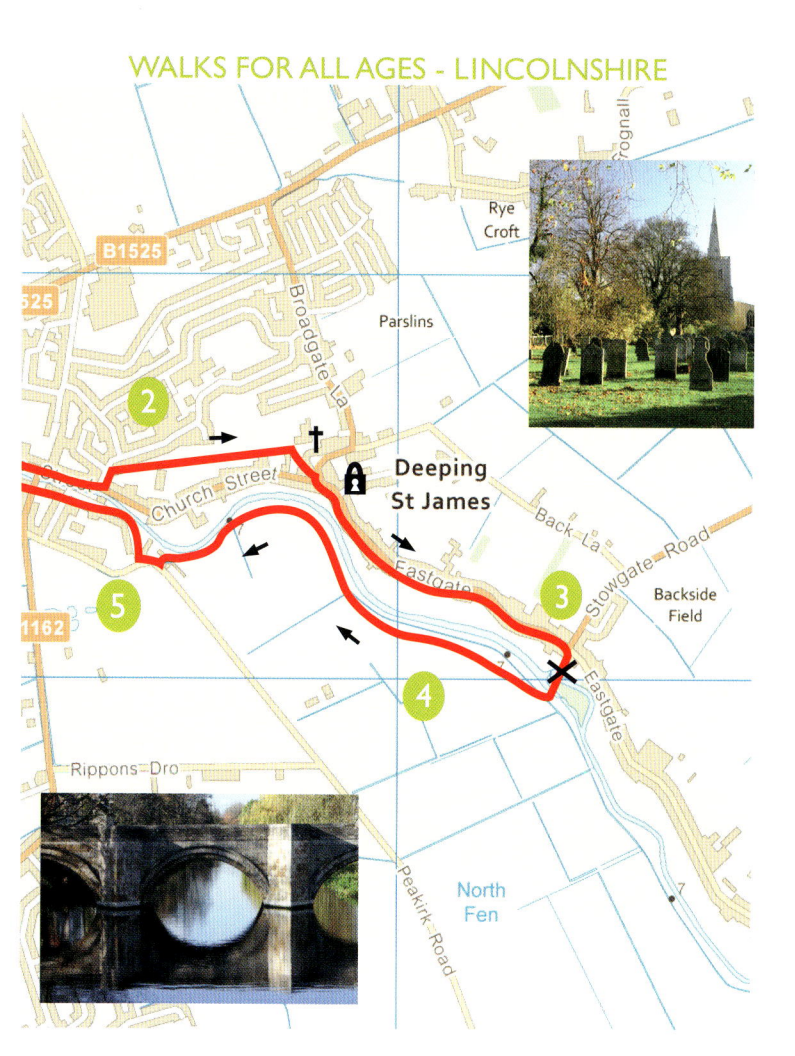

5. Walk forward for 20 yards then go right into "Riverside", soon veering left beside the river again. At the road at Deeping Gate keep ahead by the river, still along "Riverside", until the houses end. Continue across two fields (there's a footbridge between them) to reach a hand gate on your right. Cross a paddock to another gate just left of a bungalow and cross its drive to a third gate. After another paddock a fourth gate accesses a footpath through trees; continue to a road.

6. Turn right over the river back into Lincolnshire and into Market Deeping, Market Place.

St James's Church

THORNTON ABBEY

This short walk ought to be combined with a visit to the magnificent, historic Thornton Abbey – one of Lincolnshire's premier mediaeval religious sites.

The route also presents considerable contrasts between the ancient and the modern, for although heavy industry has relatively few strongholds in Lincolnshire the landscape of Thornton Abbey does have a strange juxtaposition with its backdrop of the Humber Bank oil refineries.

The abbey is probably the county's finest preserved monastic building – the only other serious rival being in the far south at Crowland. Thornton's first monks were Augustinians (or Black Canons), who came from Yorkshire to found the abbey in 1139. Keen-eyed readers will, however, notice that the Ordnance Survey gives a date of 1148. There is an explanation: the original foundation was as a priory and only nine years later was it granted "abbey" status.

The magnificent approach flanked by high, niched brick walls gives an immediate impression of the abbey's wealth and power. Closing the end stands the fifty-feet-high gatehouse that was begun about 1382 following a royal licence to "crenellate". It is built from a combination of stone and brick, the latter particularly making a clear statement of the abbey's financial status, for in the 14th century brick was a new and expensive material. Inside, a maze of rooms and passageways lead through the abbots' quarters and courtroom whilst on the second floor are turret rooms and garderobes (toilets).

Little survives of the actual church and cloisters apart from a section of the ornate, octagonal chapter house of 1282, which formed part of a wide-ranging rebuilding begun around 1264. The abbey's ground plan, however, is still easily traced and remains impressive even in its reduced state.

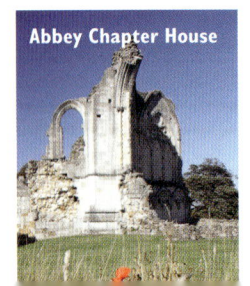

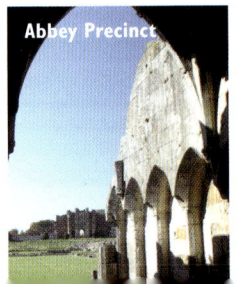

WALKS FOR ALL AGES - LINCOLNSHIRE

The property is cared for by English Heritage, which provides detailed and useful information boards and a guide. There is an admission charge for non-members and the EH website gives details of opening hours etc. Parking is available at the abbey (if you are visiting) with spare capacity along the nearby approach lane.

Just a few fields away stands the local railway station named after the abbey. The line here was opened on 1st March 1848 by the Manchester, Sheffield and Lincolnshire Railway as their link to the Humber ferry from New Holland to Hull. Unusually, two lines opened that same day: one from Lincoln and one from Louth via Grimsby, meeting at Ulceby Junction three miles away. A temporary station for Thornton, opened in November 1848, was initially built at Thornton Curtis, where the stationmaster also ran the inn. The station was later relocated to its present site and renamed in honour of the nearby abbey. The grassy lane along which we approach it was the main highway until 1885.

RAF North Killingholme was located about a mile to the south of the abbey (our route passes close to it). It was built in 1942/43 and 550 Squadron were based there throughout from that time until closure in 1945 immediately World War II had ended. The squadron suffered heavy losses: 61 aircraft and over 300 personnel in a mere three years.

THE BASICS

Distance in miles & km: 4 miles: 6.5 kilometres.
Gradient: Level.
Severity: Easy.
Approx time to walk: 120 mins.
Stiles: None.
Maps: OS Landranger 113 (Grimsby): Explorer 284.
Path description: Grass track, field paths and country lanes.
Start Point: Thornton Abbey car park. DN39 6TU (GR 115190)
Parking: Thornton Abbey.
Dog friendly: Most of the route except public roads, or fields with stock.
Public toilets: Only at abbey.
Nearest food: Drinks/Picnic site at the abbey. East Halton: Black Bull.

THORNTON ABBEY WALK

1. Walk along the lane away from the abbey gateway, and at the junction cross onto the grass track opposite. At the railway cross the lines with care and immediately take the fenced path on the left. Continue along this, parallel with the railway, for about a mile, eventually emerging from a tree-lined track by a level crossing.

2. Turn left over this and at the first road junction keep right through a double bend. (The site of the former RAF North Killingholme is to your right here.) About 200 yards after passing a pumping station turn left at a footpath sign.

3. Follow a track for just over half a mile (there's a zigzag about halfway) until you come to another footpath sign pointing to the right. Ignore this and keep ahead to a road; there are

80

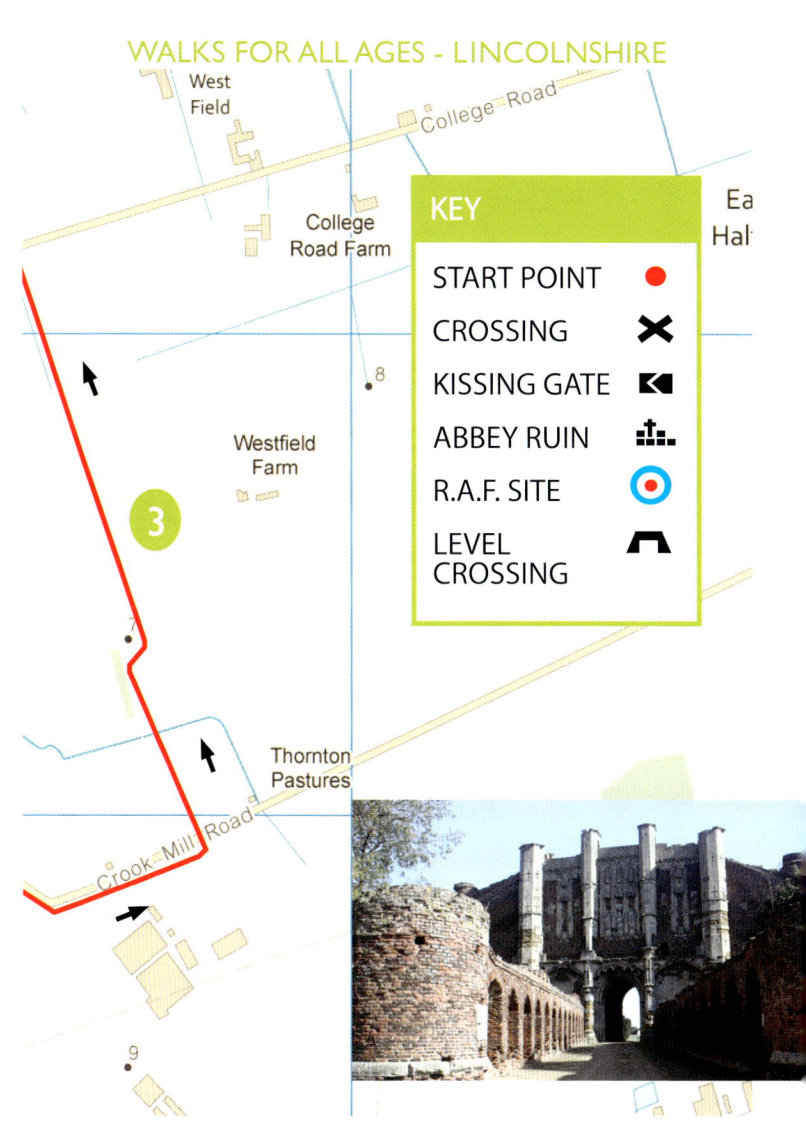

WALKS FOR ALL AGES - LINCOLNSHIRE

KEY

START POINT	●
CROSSING	✕
KISSING GATE	◁
ABBEY RUIN	⛪
R.A.F. SITE	◉
LEVEL CROSSING	⌒

fine views leftwards to Thornton Abbey across the fields here.

4. At the road turn left for 120 yards and at a right-hand bend look for a footpath with a footbridge and kissing gate in trees on your left. Once across the bridge bear right towards another footbridge and continue beyond that to a third. Cross this too and then bear left to a kissing gate and carry on with a hedge to your right and close-up views of the abbey. Go through a kissing gate and walk along to some steps down a bank that once formed part of the abbey moat. After another gate bear left diagonally over a paddock and through a final kissing gate onto a road.

5. Turn left and in 100 yards you will reach the abbey car park.

THURLBY & DOLE WOOD

Thurlby is an attractive village on the edge of the Fens just south of Bourne. Nearby Dole Wood is one of Lincolnshire's finest bluebell woods; a springtime visit is particularly recommended.

Thurlby's name originates from the Old Danish for "Thorulf's farmstead" but had become "Torolvebi" by the time of the Domesday Book (1086). The village was settled even earlier, however, something confirmed by 10th-century Anglo-Saxon masonry built into the church tower. The picturesque High Street has some 16th-century timber-framed thatched cottages.

The church's unusual dedication (with only one other in the country) is to St Firmin, the first Bishop of Amiens who was martyred in AD 303. Look in the porch to see two ancient stone coffin lids. A fine section of the Roman Car Dyke forms the western boundary of the churchyard, where there is an information board. The "Dyke" linked the rivers Nene and Witham and archaeologists are unsure whether it was primarily a drainage system or a canal for transporting goods to the Roman garrison at Lincoln and thence, via the Foss Dyke and Trent, to York. The A15 at Thurlby also follows the course of the Roman "King Street", a fenland loop off Ermine Street.

To enter Dole Wood we cross the former trackbed of the railway opened in 1860 by the Bourne and Essendine Railway Company but operated by the Great Northern Railway, who took it over completely by 1864. Bourne was eventually to become an important junction, but this was the first railway

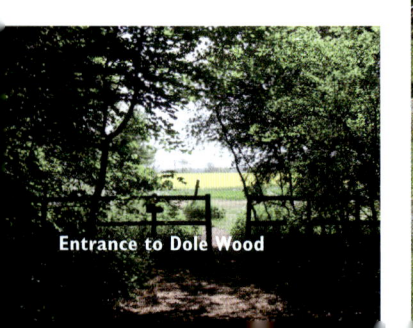

WALKS FOR ALL AGES - LINCOLNSHIRE

into the town. Its closure in June 1951 made it the first Lincolnshire railway to shut down after the war.

And so to Dole Wood itself! This is ancient woodland that probably established itself when glaciers retreated after the last ice age and would probably have formed part of an extensive forest. Since at least the 11th century it has been "managed" by man, who has repeatedly harvested and replenished its resources by coppicing – a practice that continues even today. Surrounding parts of the wood, particularly to the west and south, are traces of a boundary ditch that may also have been fenced in order to keep animals out; though sometimes such boundaries were intended to keep them in! At the time of the Domesday Book Dole Wood covered about 130 acres but it now covers only about ten. Currently leased to the Lincolnshire Wildlife Trust it is also a Site of Special Scientific Interest (SSSI) and open to the public all year round. It's best visited between mid April and early May to see the splendid display of bluebells.

THE BASICS

Distance in miles & km: 4¾ miles: 7.5 kilometres.
Gradient: Very easy – almost level.
Severity: Easy. Gentle rise to reach Dole Wood.
Approx time to walk: 120 mins.
Stiles: 5.
Maps: OS Landranger 130 (Grantham): Explorer 248.
Path description: Village pavements, grass, woodland footpaths.
Start Point: The Horseshoe inn, Thurlby. PE10 0EL (GR 104168)
Parking: The Horseshoe inn, Thurlby.
Dog friendly: On leads best throughout.
Public toilets: None.
Nearest food: The Horseshoe, Thurlby.

THURLBY WALK

1. From the inn car park cross the main road (A15) and walk up High Street into Thurlby village. Just before the chapel look for a footpath sign pointing to the left.

2. Turn here and walk past a large corrugated-iron shed to a kissing gate and then keep ahead in a meadow beside a hedge to a stile and footbridge in the far corner. Continue along a grass path as a ditch develops on the right; cross this at a footbridge. Next veer half left over an arable field to a stile and footbridge near some metal gates. Maintain your direction over a meadow to another stile visible on the skyline then cross a final field to a footpath sign at a road (Obthorpe Lane). Turn sharply right back along this lane until you reach the Dole Wood noticeboard.

3. Dole Wood entrance is up the adjacent track. Explore the wood at your leisure or follow my recommended route.

4. Just inside turn right and cross a footbridge, then go left along the path beside the former railway. In approximately 300 yards turn left over a second bridge and walk up the perimeter of a more open grass area to find a viewpoint seat at the hilltop. Just beyond this veer right into the woods where a path leads to a footbridge and then divides. Going either way leads back to the entrance. Then return to the road.

5. Now bear left and at the road junction in Thurlby village turn right. (You can now return down High Street to the inn.)

6. Alternatively turn left at Chapel Lane into a housing estate and look for a footpath on the right by house number 14. Behind the house garden turn right and then left at the field corner. Follow the path down towards the A15, ignoring any side paths as you go. From a footbridge go right, then left to reach the road.

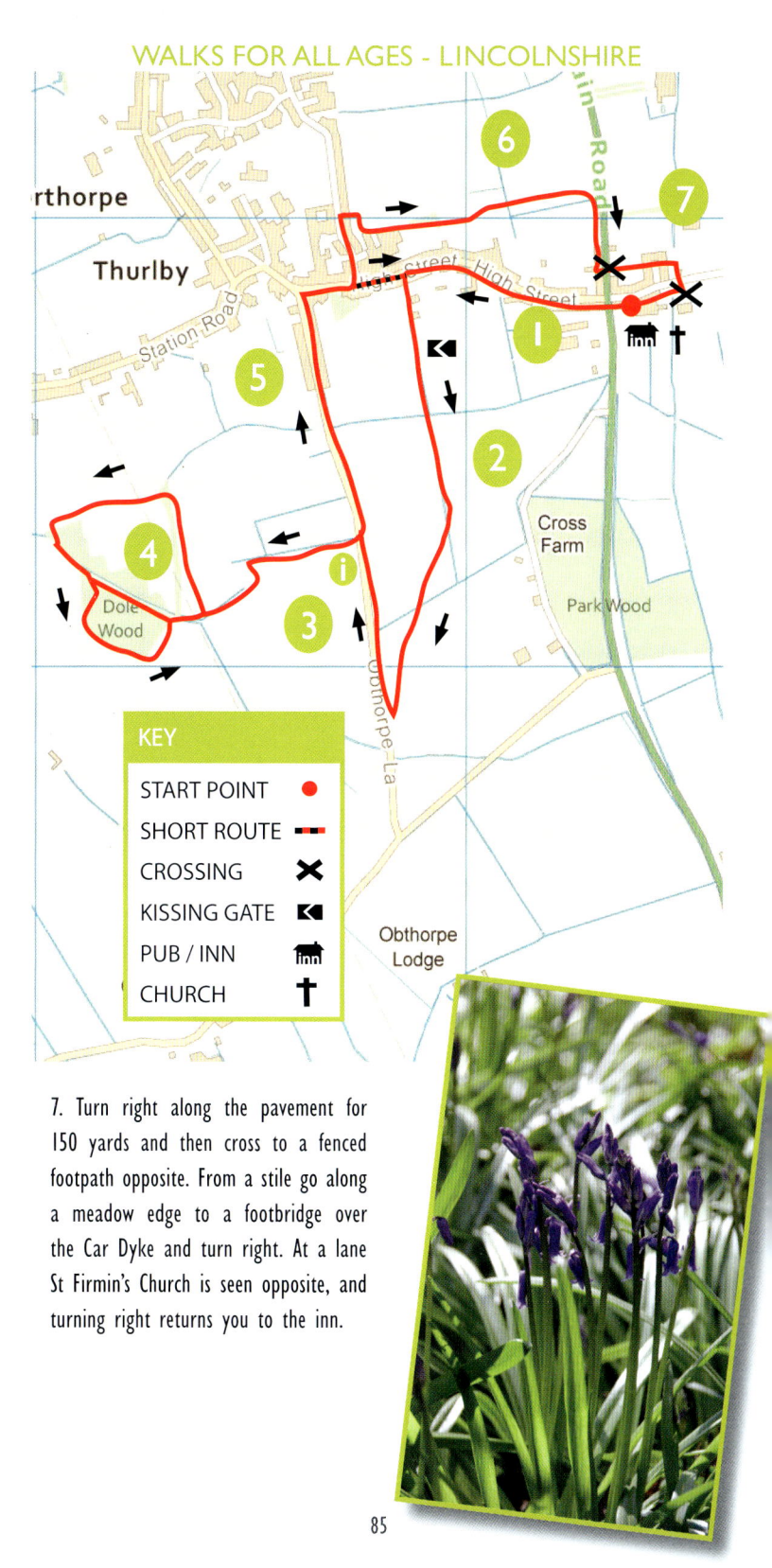

WALKS FOR ALL AGES - LINCOLNSHIRE

KEY

- START POINT ●
- SHORT ROUTE ▬▬
- CROSSING ✕
- KISSING GATE ◂◂
- PUB / INN 🏠
- CHURCH ✝

7. Turn right along the pavement for 150 yards and then cross to a fenced footpath opposite. From a stile go along a meadow edge to a footbridge over the Car Dyke and turn right. At a lane St Firmin's Church is seen opposite, and turning right returns you to the inn.

WELL & RIGSBY

This walk provides either a short outing or something slightly longer for the more confident and adventurous. Both have fine views. An optional extension also visits Well Church.

There are sweeping views down over Alford and the coastal marsh from Rigsby churchyard and the lane on the shorter route back to Well. The longer walk climbs even higher and benefits from views to the north as well.

The tiny village of Well has, in the shape of St Margaret's, one of Lincolnshire's loveliest little Georgian churches. Set high on a hilltop it is aligned, not east to west as is usual, but with Well Vale Hall below. (There's an optional short detour to visit it.)

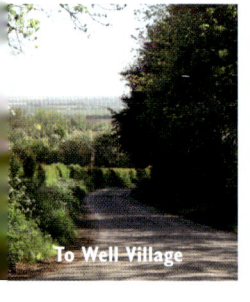

St Margaret's Church

To Well Village

Beyond Well the walk briefly follows an old railway line on the outskirts of Alford. It once linked Grimsby to Peterborough and was built by the Great Northern Railway Company to great celebrations when Alford station opened on 3rd September 1848. There were celebrations too, though much more subdued, when the station closed on 3rd October 1970 and Alford Town Band played the "Last Post".

Rigsby stands high on the eastern slopes of the Wolds and its Old Norse name means "the village on the ridge". It has had a church since Saxon times but the present one, dating from 1863, cost £685 to build — to which local farm labourers contributed a week's wages — and was designed by Louth architect James Fowler in Victorian Gothic style. Inside is a picture of its thatched predecessor and a 15th-century sword and helmet found in the churchyard.

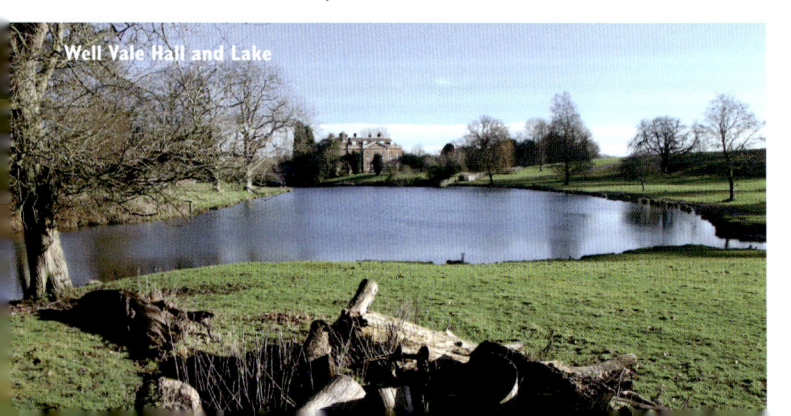

Well Vale Hall and Lake

WALKS FOR ALL AGES - LINCOLNSHIRE

An interesting feature on the short route, though superficially unremarkable, is the A1104 crossroads at Miles Cross (GR 435746). Alford was stricken by the plague in 1630/31 and, like the more famous Eyam in Derbyshire, decided to isolate itself from the outside world. The town's population was probably less than a thousand, but there were 160 deaths within just a few months. Provisions were left outside the town and payment was left in hollowed-out stones filled with vinegar as disinfectant. One of these was at Miles Cross. (The longer walk misses this but readers approaching the start from the A16 at Ulceby Cross would turn here anyway.)

Entrance to Well Vale Woods

Well Vale Woods in Winter

Rigsby Church

THE BASICS

Distance in miles & km: 4¼ or 6¼ miles: 6.75 or 10 kilometres.
Gradient: Moderate descent to Well and climb back to Rigsby.
Severity: Easy/Moderate.
Approx time to walk: (Short) 130 mins. (Longer) 200/230 mins.
Stiles: (Short) 2: (Long) 4: (Extension) adds 1.
Maps: Landranger 122 (Skegness): Explorer 274.
Path description: Country lanes, field paths, meadows, woodland.
Start Point: Well High Lane (at the bend) LN13 0EU. (GR 443737)
Parking: At start.
Dog friendly: On leads where stock may be present.
Public toilets: None.
Nearest food: None on route. Inns, cafés and tearooms in Alford.

WELL & RIGSBY MAP

1. Walk downhill into Well. (The optional extension – see (8) below – departs to the right after 350 yards.) Keep forward at the "T" junction and in a further quarter of a mile take the signed track on the left; this soon bears right to reach a metal kissing gate at the old railway embankment.

2. Bear left along this, keeping ahead where paths go off to the right. Immediately before a red gate turn left along a wide grass track to the road near a house. Cross and turn left, then in 25 yards take the footpath signed "To Rigsby".

3. From the second footbridge continue on the far side of the hedge. At the next footbridge by a copse there's a dogleg (and a seat); at the fourth footbridge enter a meadow with a four-way signpost in front of you. Turn left

88

WALKS FOR ALL AGES - LINCOLNSHIRE

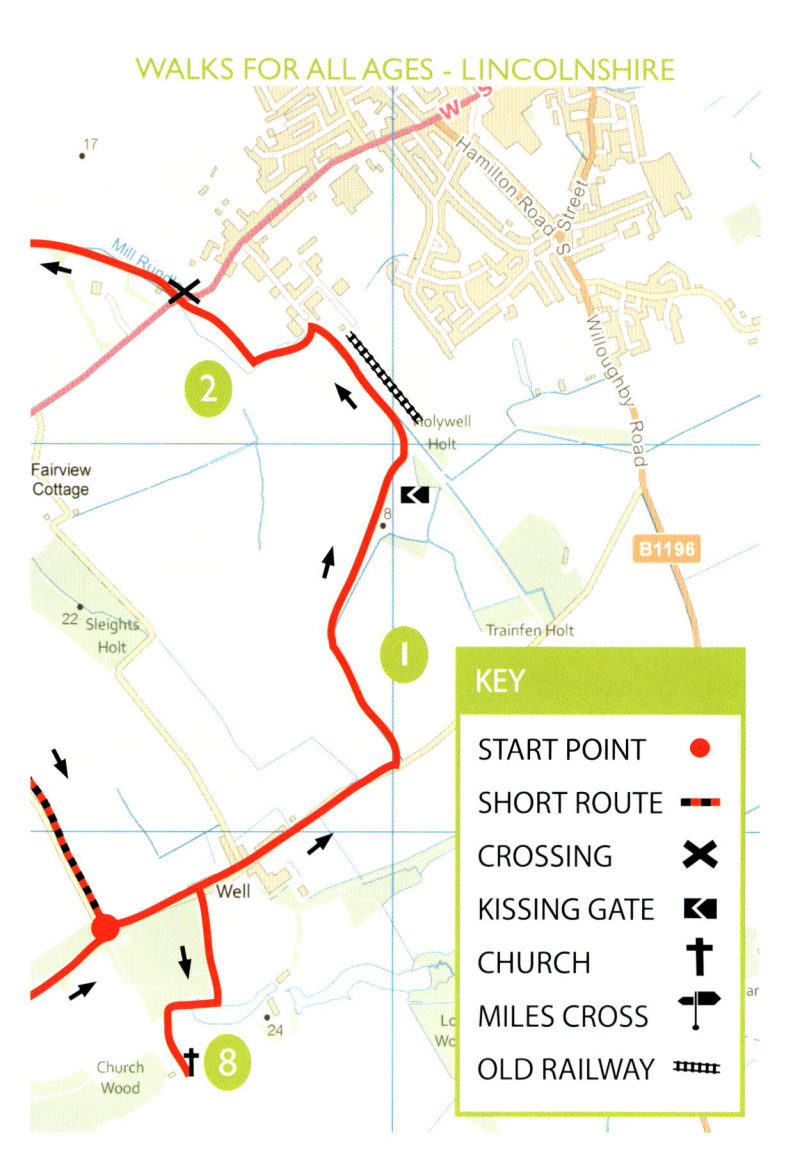

KEY

- START POINT — ●
- SHORT ROUTE — ▰▰▰
- CROSSING — ✕
- KISSING GATE — ◨
- CHURCH — ✝
- MILES CROSS — ⚑
- OLD RAILWAY — ▭▭▭

up this meadow to a stile at the top (just right of centre) and then veer left past the church to a road.

4. [SHORT ROUTE] This goes left following the road to Miles Cross, over the main road and along the lane opposite back to the start.

5. [THE LONGER ROUTE] For this turn right for 200 yards to a signed uphill track on the left and where this ends follow the field-edge path by the hedge on your right. After left and right turns the path swings left again to join a road by a house.

6. The path continues in the woods opposite and keeps alongside the perimeter fence for a quarter of a mile to a stile. Climb this and cross a meadow heading towards the right-hand end of the trees ahead. At

WELL & RIGSBY WALK

another stile join a track and turn right towards a farm. At the farmyard another track goes off to the left. Follow this past a copse and ahead over field on a well-defined grass strip.

7. At a footpath sign enter Well Vale Woods, join a track and bear left. Ignore any side tracks and you will eventually reach a gate at the road where you began.

8. [OPTIONAL EXTENSION] Near the start, as you approach Well village, there is a stile on the right. Climb over and walk by woods for about 300 yards until you can turn right again. Beyond the lake bear left over grass and up a short, steep climb to the Georgian-style St Margaret's Church where the porch offers more fine views. Return the same way.

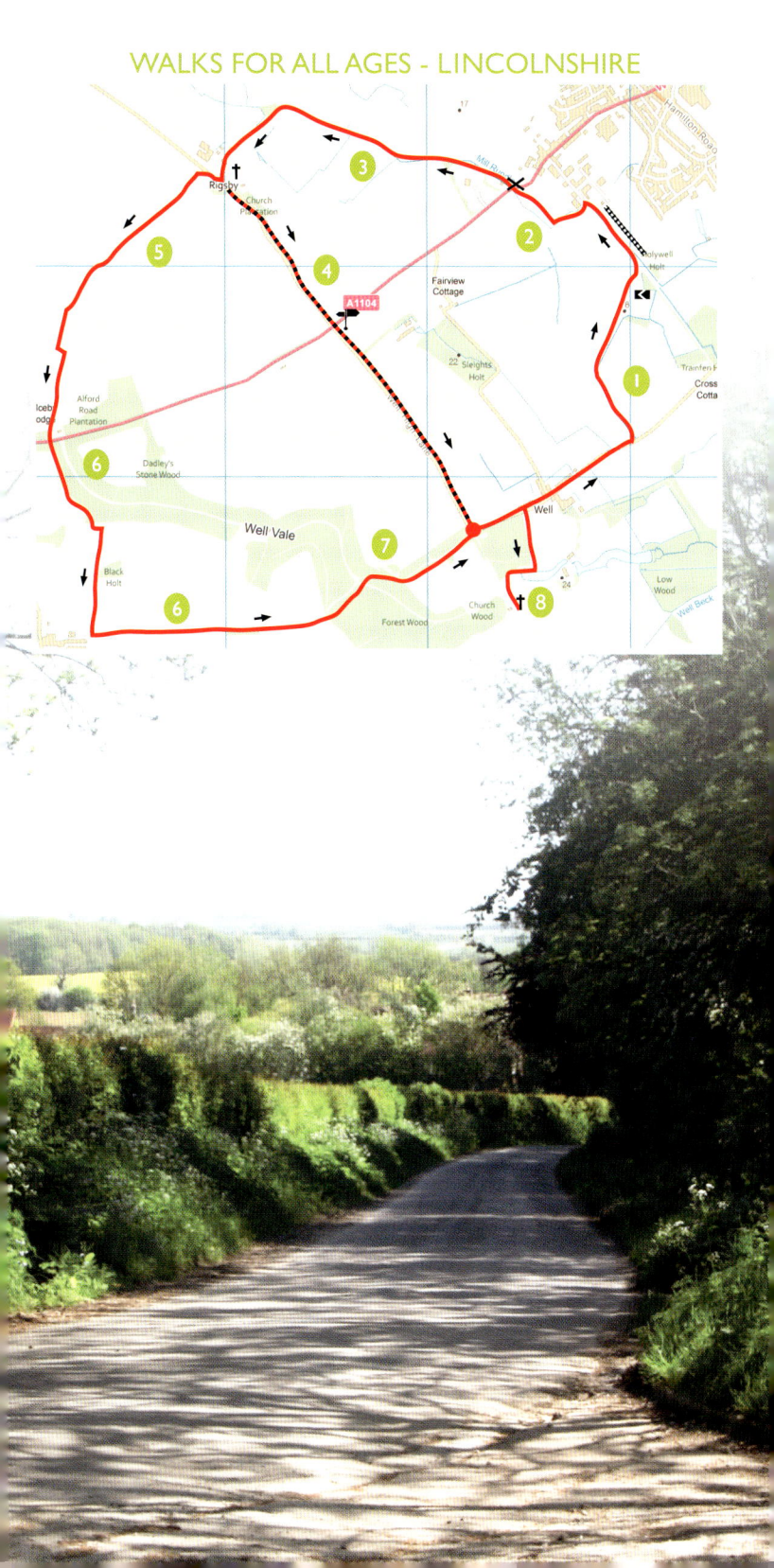

WALKS FOR ALL AGES - LINCOLNSHIRE

WOOLSTHORPE

This walk near the Lincolnshire/Leicestershire border explores the valley of the River Devon at Woolsthorpe and returns along the Viking Way beside the Grantham Canal.

This 33-mile-long canal links the town via the Vale of Belvoir to the River Trent at Nottingham. Construction, begun in 1793, took four years, but once opened the canal proved a boon to Grantham's prosperity and remained so for over 50 years until the first railway (the Ambergate, Nottingham, Boston and Eastern Junction Railway Co. – the ANBEJR) reached the town in 1851. Trade then decreased until the ANBEJR was absorbed by the Great Northern Railway (GNR), who saw the canal as a rival and allowed further gradual decline, something hastened by increasing competition from road transport. Traffic temporarily increased during the First World War but the canal's closure became unavoidable by 1929.

Ironstone was first quarried locally in the 1870s near Woolsthorpe at Brewers Grave, behind the woods to the south of the inn, with the ore carried by tramway down to Woolsthorpe Wharf and shipped out by barges. Production soon outstripped the canal's capacity and in 1883 a branch line from Belvoir Junction to Woolsthorpe was opened. This soon evolved into an extensive railway system as further deposits were exploited as far away as Denton, Harlaxton and Stroxton. When quarrying ceased in 1974 so of course did the raison d'être of the railway but the old embankments, where today's cycleway begins near Lock 18 (Woolsthorpe Top), show where the line crossed the canal.

The present-day hamlet of Stenwith was a substantial village in mediaeval times and in the Domesday Book of 1086 nineteen freemen and their families were recorded. Although the mediaeval village has now disappeared the OS map shows a moat site, but it is unseen from the walk.

The final part of the walk from Muston Bridge (Number 59) follows the towpath, which after Stenwith Bridge (Number 60) coincides with the Viking Way. Of particular interest here is the number of locks passed. The first is Lock 12, immediately after Muston Bridge, which marks the end of a 20-mile pound (i.e. a lock-free section of canal), the previous lock being beside the Fosse Way (A46) in Nottinghamshire. From there the canal's route was skilfully engineered to follow the natural contours of the Vale of Belvoir. Lock 12 (Woolsthorpe Bottom Lock) is also the first of the Woolsthorpe Flight, seven locks, numbered twelve to eighteen, all within two miles, which raised the canal about 59 feet. When built each one cost £950 including all labour and materials.

Towards the end of the walk the buildings known as the "Carpenter's Shop" are seen on the opposite bank. These comprised a workshop and stores for canal maintenance together with offices and stables and were restored in 1994.

The Dirty Duck Inn (or Rutland Arms), where our walk starts, also dates from the time of the canal's heyday when it was much frequented by the bargemen. It is signposted down a side lane just north of Woolsthorpe-by-Belvoir village. Readers may use the inn car park but are asked to patronise the inn in appreciation.

THE BASICS

Distance in miles & km: 3 or 3¾ miles: 5 or 6 kilometres.
Gradient: Level throughout.
Severity: Easy.
Approx time to walk: 90 mins.
Stiles: 4.
Maps: OS Landranger 130 (Grantham): Explorer 247.
Path description: Country lanes, field paths, canal towpath.
Start Point: Rutland Arms (Dirty Duck), Woolsthorpe.
Parking: At Rutland Arms.
Dog friendly: Best on leads.
Public toilets: None.
Nearest food: Rutland Arms (Dirty Duck)

WOOLSTHORPE WALK

1. From the inn walk back down the approach lane to the road, cross over and turn left along the pavement. Near the edge of Woolsthorpe village, close to the 30 mph speed limit sign, double back down steps to take the signed field path on the right. Cross an arable field (the path is usually well marked) keeping forward through a hedge and maintaining the same line over a second field and reach a farm track at the far side.

2. Cross this and continue along a grassy field edge with the little River Devon now on your left. Keep close to the river until the path enters some trees and reaches an old brick bridge. Cross this and turn right along the river's opposite bank. Continue over several stiles, always near the river, until after a final meadow you reach a stile at a road.

3. [SHORT CUT] Turn right here and follow the road to the canal bridge. On the far side keep forward 100 yards then double back sharply to the left where a path through trees reaches the towpath. Then, on joining the longer route, turn left.

4. [LONGER ROUTE] Turn left along the road for about half a mile to the canal at Muston Bridge, cross the canal and turn right onto the towpath.

5. A delightful canal-side stroll of 1½ miles now returns you to Woolsthorpe Wharf. Just beyond the bridge (Number 61) you can visit the final two locks of the Woolsthorpe Flight. Return over the canal bridge to the Rutland Arms.

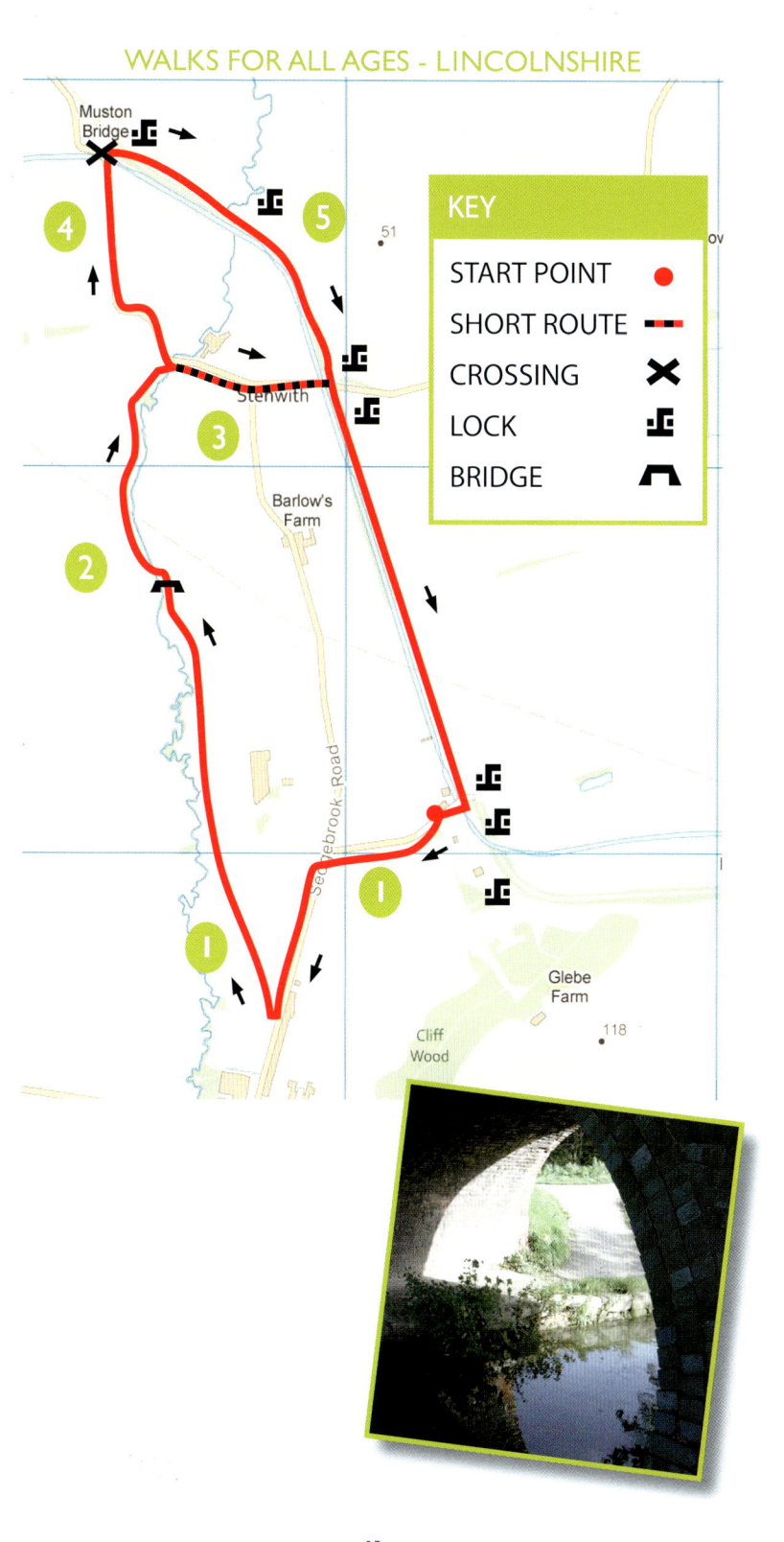

WALKS FOR ALL AGES - LINCOLNSHIRE

KEY

- START POINT ●
- SHORT ROUTE ▬ ▬
- CROSSING ✗
- LOCK
- BRIDGE ⌒

ABOUT THE AUTHOR

Hugh Marrows has lived in Lincolnshire all his life. He is married with two grown-up children.

His working life was spent in the civil service, where for many years his job involved a great deal of travelling throughout the county, and it is from that time that he developed his interest in Lincolnshire's diverse landscape, architecture and all aspects of its history and heritage.

With a long-standing love of the outdoors and an interest in photography he naturally came to appreciate the visual archaeological heritage that Lincolnshire offers, in addition to its churches, vernacular buildings and the industrial legacy of its mills, canals and long-lost railways.

He was fortunate to be able to obtain early retirement from his civil service career — something that allowed him both time and opportunity to pursue his interests more fully. It was then that he decided to turn them to advantage by writing about them — initially for a county magazine — to encourage others to explore the county for themselves, and before long he also found himself writing for local newspapers. He has also done freelance work for various publications produced by Lincolnshire County Council.

Over the years all this has led to him having several books published including a guide to the Viking Way for Lincolnshire County Council, two books devoted to walks on the Lincolnshire Wolds, and two others of general walks throughout the county plus one based entirely around the Grantham Canal.

His other interests include watercolour painting, travel and jazz.